Notes on Living
Reflections on Ukraine Today

Edited by Max Eulitz

With contributions by

Mariana Berezovska
Oksana Briukhovetska
Oleksandr Burlaka
Davyd Chychkan
Hixto
Yelizaveta Landenberger
Yuliia Leites
Oleksii Minko
Marharyta Polovinko
Julia Stakhivska
Nastya Vogan
Arina Yanovych

Foreword

Max Eulitz

My route to Ukraine? Via Russia, of all places.

On a balmy evening in late summer 2017, I sat with a group of self-proclaimed anarchists around a campfire in the small village of Prjamuchino, somewhere in the middle of nowhere between St. Petersburg and Moscow. A deserted stretch of land, full of mosquitoes and cheap booze.

On the occasion of the Russian Revolution's centennial anniversary, like-minded thinkers gathered here, at the birthplace of Mikhail Bakunin—the notorious revolutionary and founder of anarchism—for a multi-day conference. An event that mainly consisted of tediously long lectures and never ending walks through the surrounding wheat fields.

According to my interpreter, the theme of the meeting was "Anarchists against Anarchy and Anarchism."

The atmosphere was somewhat informal. Most of the participants knew each other. It was a diverse group of women and men of different ages. We bunked together in an abandoned school. During the day, we listened. In the evening, we drank and debated. This meeting posed no threat to the state, and yet a very similar gathering had been attacked a year earlier. Young neo-Nazis with connections to the Kremlin had stormed the conference venue. As a result, one participant lost an eye.

Still, the symposium met again that summer. There, in Prjamunchino, intellectual radicals, chronic refusers, misfits, and hopeless optimists assembled. People very much to my liking, who still believed in this country despite the regime's reprisals, despite the murders of journalists and opposition figures, despite the attacks on neighboring states. My diary entry from August 15, 2017, reads:

Around the campfire: socialist poems and anarchist battle cries. As long as there are people like this, there is hope for this country.

Today, I no longer have such hope. Even in knowing the atrocities committed against the Ukrainian population, no one in Russia is taking to the streets. There is no civil disobedience, no protest, no visible resistance. The wannabe revolutionaries have fled into exile or have fallen silent in defeat. The rest of the human warmth seems to have escaped from this huge, cold body.

Fact is, if only a third of the Russian population stopped working tomorrow and stayed at home, the war could be over the day after tomorrow. Instead, indifference has triumphed. The immutability of the existing conditions now seems to be the driving force behind social activity.

Today's Ukraine appears the exact opposite. Here, the full complexity of a free society is on display. Even though this freedom is restricted by the fact that the country is under hostile siege, self-determined individuals are engaged in an active civil society. There is discourse, demonstrations, freedom of speech, and freedom of press.

In the summer of 2018, I flew to Kyiv for the first time. Although the purpose of my residency at the Goethe-Institut was to research Soviet monuments, I did not stick to this plan for long. Instead, I shifted my focus onto "living" places—monuments in fluid form, bastions of civil engagement. So I ended up writing a book about the construction of a techno club that would soon become a cultural institution, K41. A place of lived diversity, an expression of the country's openness, which ultimately also took on responsibility in times of war.

Without wanting to sugarcoat the dramatic situation, Putin's campaign has clearly missed its main objective. Instead of a suppressed colony under the yoke of an imperialist regime, Ukraine remains an independent state with empowered citizens.

Building on this insight, this publication attempts to formulate a vision for the future through reflections on the present. For the future of Ukraine will not be decided on the battlefield alone. Extreme situations put societies to the test. Centrifugal forces from all directions pull at their internal structure. That is why it is important, despite the tense situation and polarization, to lay the groundwork for a progressive, open society.

A legitimate successor to Bakunin—both in spirit and in action—was the Ukrainian, Nestor Makhno. Born in 1888, he followed in the footsteps of his ideological mentor, and at least temporarily, realized what the latter had only dared to dream of. In the turmoil of the Russian Civil War between 1919 and 1923, he took control, ad interim, of a large part of Ukraine, and implemented collective organization through councils based upon anarchist principles. In addition to strengthening local self-government, it was above all his rejection of an authoritarian state, and his resistance to military dictatorship, that continues to resonate today.

The Progressive Core

Davyd Chychkan's drawings clearly show that this political stance has, once again, gained relevance in the face of an imperialist war of aggression. They depict portraits of Ukrainian and international left-wing fighters—anarchists and socialists—who joined the military resistance against the Russian attack and occupation. Chychkan himself was an anarcho-syndicalist and anti-fascist. During the large-scale invasion, the established artist declined invitations from international institutions and refused to travel abroad, even temporarily.

In the summer of 2024, he stopped working on this series to voluntarily join the 241st Mortar Battery of the Kyiv Brigade. A year later, on August 9, 2025, he was fatally wounded by a Russian FPV drone during a combat mission.

In one of his last interviews, he said:

I voluntarily conscripted into the army as a soldier because I have left-wing political views. This means I am against exclusivity: I believe that I am no different from peasants, teachers, or the proletariat. I refuse my privilege as an artist, including traveling abroad.

For him, an active public stance and political awareness were inseparable from his artistic practice.

Ukraine is a modern national project with a leftist and anti-authoritarian basis [...] I believe that it is possible to prevent the victory of neoliberals and neoconservatives and return modern Ukraine to the project that was conceived by Ukrainian modernists. [...] Ukraine is a progressive project at its core, a project against oppression.

External Structures

This modernization project is undoubtedly also being negotiated in the field of architecture. In his "War Time City Guide," architect and Maidan photographer Sasha Burlaka (p. 106) describes how urban structures are adapting to the war, and what challenges city dwellers will continue to face even after the war ends. He also

takes the funeral of Davyd Chychkan as an example
to describe new forms of remembrance culture.

Kyiv-born architect Arina Yanovych (p. 78) takes
a similarly forward-looking perspective. In her contribution, she addresses Kyiv's garage culture—community
spaces birthed in the city's hundreds of parking garages.
This very Eastern European achievement could serve as
a microcosm and model for urban society as a whole—
outside of capitalist imperatives. Her plea: after the wild
construction boom of the 1990s, during which time
real estate investors were the driving force behind urban
development, it is now time for urban planning with clear
regulations, and a prioritization of solidarity in everyday
life. Through the prism of pragmatism, she sees guide-
lines for a successful community that puts the interests
of the investor class behind the needs of the residents.

However, interpersonal networks only work when
a common language is found. So not surprisingly, language policy is currently a hot topic for many Ukrainians.
Since the full-scale invasion, but also long before that,
language has been used as a means of exercising
power, exclusion, and oppression. Mariana Berezovska
(p. 24) addresses this controversial matter in her essay,
"The Language Question."

The self-perception of Ukrainian identity and feelings of belonging as a sovereign nation are inextricably
linked to an alliance with Western values. Nonetheless,
the partially euphoric orientation toward the West
after the Maidan Revolution has suffered a setback due
to the lack of, or if only half-hearted support, since the
outbreak of the war. Yelizaveta Landenberger (p. 96)
attempts to determine why the so-called West finds
it so difficult to support this country unconditionally,
and with all its might.

A similarly challenging perspective is offered in the text by Нixто (p. 46), which translates as "Nobody." The anonymous author describes their years of work in Kyiv, to create a *third space* beyond national and gender binaries, an architecture that facilitates freedom and belonging. The text critically reflects on how debates around authenticity and questions of legitimacy influenced their work. Нixто argues that true inclusion requires structural safeguards and a legal framework, as well as a willingness to tolerate differences. The author issues a strong warning about the pitfalls of identity politics and nationalist tendencies.

Inner Structures

Switching from an external to an internal perspective, Yuliia Leites (p. 38), a psychoanalytic psychotherapist, shares experiences from therapy sessions with soldiers and their families. The text accompanies a Ukrainian serviceman and his recurring dreams of impending death and survival. The text refers to autopoiesis, a form of self-preservation through retreat and renewal, and illustrates how sleep, omission, and abandonment serve as protective pauses that preserve feelings in wartime.

Oleksii Minko (p. 86) also makes use of dreams in his autofictional writing. Reminiscent of magical realism, this narrative style interweaves his personal experiences during the occupation of his hometown, Berdyansk, with reports from friends, relatives and news organisations. Minko's contribution illustrates the surreal living conditions and challenges experienced under foreign rule.

This shift towards introversion, and a heightened sensoriality is also evident in the work of the poet

Julia Stakhivska (pp. 23, 37, 61, 85). The poems in this publication bear witness to a transformative change in awareness, in a landscape of military escalation. Her evocative verses encourage us to sharpen our senses in an irrevocably altered world. She challenges us to cut through the noise of war.

Similarly subjective yet rooted in rolling facts, Ukranian DJ, Nastya Vogan (p. 14) reflects on her life between three homes: Odesa, Kyiv, and Berlin. With her relentless eye for transgressions and atmospheric nuances, she makes it clear through her observations in transit spaces that empathy and decency need no boundaries, and that individual freedom has more value when shared.

The artist Marharyta Polovinko certainly shared this unconditional notion of freedom. Throughout the book, her haunting drawings confront the horrors of a man-made hell. By using unconventional materials such as her own blood, or dry ink pens to scratch images into paper, her works denounce the *conditio humana*, as they testify to an untenable situation.

After the outbreak of war, she volunteered in the southern regions of Mykolaiv and Kherson, helping to rebuild homes that had been destroyed by Russian bombs. Later, she worked as part of a CASEVAC team responsible for medical evacuation under fire.

In an interview in November 2023, she says:

Art usually exists in places where it is hard to live without it. With the war, there has been more art in my life, yet with it came the understanding that I could not do anything with this art. I can neither sell it nor give it away because it is blood, it is pain, it is suffering. This is the kind of material for which there is no place, I don't even want it to exist. It is valuable now because it works as a mirror of reality, but I want the moment to come when it stops reflecting this world.

In the fall of 2024, she eventually joined the 2nd Mechanized Battalion of the 3rd Separate Assault Brigade, where she served as a drone pilot. Marharyta died on the front lines during a combat mission on April 5, 2025.

Marharyta Polovinko's use of blood as an artistic medium is addressed by Oksana Briukhovetska (p. 62) in her essay, "On Blood and the Most Radical Gesture of Care." In it, she elaborates upon several local artistic practices in Kyiv, each uniquely addressing personal and political crises, and particularly focusing on the role of female-run art-venues and apartment exhibitions as cultural safe spaces.

Ukraine's freedom comes at a high price. It always has. Nestor Machno fought all his life for Ukrainian autonomy. To him, fighting the "Ruski Mir"—the concept of "Greater Russia"—whether under Tsarist or Bolshevik rule, was a battle against imperial ambitions. And the one thing imperial and autocratic regimes fear most is independent thought and action. Shortly before his death in French exile in 1934, he wrote:

The freedom of each individual carries within it the seed of a free society. ●

Max Eulitz is an artist and writer based in Berlin. In 2022 he published *Notes on 41*, a collection of essays illustrating the circumstances surrounding the creation of a nightclub in Kyiv.

Points of Destination

Nastya Vogan

Skimming through my notes, I'm writing this from the enveloping, muted safety of my second home, Berlin. The room is silent and somnolent—my own state has drifted into the same quietness in recent weeks—probably a delayed payment for the intensity I experienced in my first home, Ukraine. Each journey is its own contribution to keeping the connection intact.

Due to Russian aerial attacks and broken flight corridors, Ukraine has entered another dimension of the global geo-temporal field. What used to be a barely noticeable hour and a half flight now takes more than twenty-four hours. Switching between trains—the same amount of time it takes to travel to Tasmania. The distance hasn't changed; only the route's architecture has: detours, layovers, and redirected airspace. The body learns this new remoteness through waiting rooms and security lines, and through the slow accumulation of hours that bring you to the edge of the map.

Moving between these two places never feels linear. It's more like transitioning through a membrane, drifting between different zones of pressure. Travel becomes not simply a route, but a state: the world narrows into train corridors, border lights, overheated compartments, and soft vibrations. A topology of motion where my body shifts its weight with each subtle change in direction. In this liminal space, the concepts of departure and permanence cease to be opposites, and instead become manifestations of a shared underlying current.

Freedom Routines

I deeply cherish my privilege of being able to witness both here and there. Though, my ability to move freely between countries is not shared by others. Either

current laws forbid it, or their hands can't unclench.
Invisible magnets glue people to places.

Friends who volunteer in evacuations from the
front line territories told me about psychological phe-
nomena where residents refuse to leave their ruined
homes, reasoning that they have a flower garden
to water. Blossoming Ukrainian gardens tended by
grandmothers, full of marigolds and mallows.

In recent history, no modern nation has lived this
long within an ongoing catastrophe while still remaining whole and functioning. In Ukraine, war permeates morning routines. A society that works, studies,
creates, and loves—all while under attack.

So, when daily confrontation with destruction
becomes the background condition, the psyche's
defence mechanisms are stretched to the extreme.

It's impossible for a human to fully comprehend
even one death—then how can we cope with death
multiplied? Death seems always close, as a thought,
as a probability, as an occurrence—with no end in sight.

And yet, there is barely room to reflect on what
is still unfolding. Russian drones and missile attacks
continue, and become more inventive.

I suspect the body keeps a more accurate record
of war than memory does. It recalls every air raid as
a tightening under the ribs, every blackout as temporary
blindness and loss of control, and every departure as
a shift in pulse—a personal archive of micro-tensions.

Falling Asleep, Counting Drones

Every night in Kyiv, I fall asleep wearing a pendant. It's
two metal wardrobe tokens from the club[1] on a chain.
One has the number 2666, and the other has the ♯
symbol. That way, they can identify my body if a rocket

Points of Destination

hits my house. The probability is low, but not zero. I first received the token as a gift, it was designed by a friend and it became the *kleynody*[2] of my residence.

The warm chain and pendant against my skin remind me of my own mortality. Ritual becomes an infrastructure of intimacy with death, which is inevitable and cannot be ignored. Every affection rehearses disappearance—there's no clear line between libido and mortido; one leaks into the other like warmth into metal. Can this moment be shared without experiencing it?

There is a certain quality to the existential thoughts of people who spend sleepless nights listening to explosions in the sky. During an air raid, weird thoughts start to enter your mind. This is especially true if you're alone. When you can't manage to fall asleep before it starts, or you're waking up from its howl, "It's a time in your life when you ask yourself a series of questions—am I happy with who I am? Or am I just living?"[3]

Explosions. One, two. Three. Their rhythm is uncertain and jarring.

You can soften the edge with the presence of a warm entity, like a cat or a neighbour.

Pressure makes diamonds, they say.

Soft Infrastructure

It's fascinating how connections fracture. Instead of coming together over shared values, we often divide over disagreements, defining ourselves by what we refuse to resemble.

As a teenager, I was terrified by the thought that people could never truly understand each other. Since empathy is usually based on shared experiences, it's impossible to perceive things the same way if that's not the case. Therefore, you can't re-model it to understand.

You can see colors differently and still name them the same. Does that mean society is merely a constellation of solitary universes that never collide, as Huxley[4] wrote? Does it matter if we see color the same way when we both call it our favorite?

Loneliness has been named a global epidemic, yet togetherness has become a limited resource, distributed unevenly like electricity during wartime.

Sometimes I imagine warmth as an unstable infrastructure, like the unreliable power grid. People carrying flickering generators inside them, enough to warm a room, a call, a memory. What if this is the real infrastructure we unconsciously built: a soft network of attention, care, and reminders—tiny beacons that hold us together while geography falls apart?

Homes Place

A large cloud is drifting toward me. Hey, Dad, we're at war! Can you imagine?

I'm in our empty family home in Odesa for the first time in four years. I'm overwhelmed by the southern comfort of it all.

My warm city, my dear rose, a tender dot on a map. I see Czech hedgehogs and women in shimmering swimsuits on the beach. Some things never change. Seawater still leaves salty traces on the skin that dry quickly under the sun. The living bodies of the beach glowing with dark tan, salt and light, while a few kilometers away the dead sea of Kuyalnyk keeps thinning out. It feels sacred in a way no temple ever could, but even the ecological landscape becomes a casualty in this war. Another Odesa diamond dims.

I kept moving farther away, but it was easier to leave when home still meant safety.

Yet, the concept of home is constantly shifting—expanding, shrinking, dissolving. Odesa, Kyiv, Berlin—each place holds something special, and none of them cancel each other out. I used to think I had one home, then two, but now it has become a constellation of places that claim me even when I no longer fully belong to them. Perhaps that's why movement is painful—because every arrival is also a slight betrayal of another place.

Inner Borders

In this expanded way of living, I continue to learn the new physics of borders. I learn which ones allow the body to pass without question, which one cuts dry, and which ones imitate softness while concealing a sharp edge.

In Berlin, I sit on the glittering Landwehr Canal in Kreuzberg, bathed in the late sunlight. A police boat emerges and glides solemnly toward me. It passes by, followed by five or six smaller kayaks. "Freedom of movement is everybody's right!" a protester shouts through a megaphone. Other demonstrators drift by, chanting, "No border, no nation! Stop deportation!"

Their voices echo off the water and dissolve into the wind. It feels sincere and off, slightly misplaced, like some kind of choreography from a movie scene. I watch and think about everyone who was dragged across borders against their will. I think about borders that are no longer just a metaphor when they are trampled upon by a foreign army. "Respect my borders," I think.

The protesters on the boats chant, "Let Fortress Europe fall!" I curl up, thinking of my friends defending my borders, freedom, and rights. They have no other choice, yet they still make this choice. Where do the walls of the European fortress end? How can these kind people be so numb? Meanwhile, I'm glad that it is possible for them, given that generations of protesters paved the way.

10999

Once again, I am returning from Kyiv, covered in the dust of travel, smells of diesel, instant coffee, and someone else's perfume. My skin is sticky from twenty-six hours of transit. Trains feel like temporary, slightly neglected houses on wheels. Sometimes, conductors adorn them with odd, pagan-like ritual objects. Once on a train ride, in a narrow grey, metal-walled bathroom, I counted twenty-two ornate aroma sachets arranged like charms. A carriage becomes a womb, a corridor of transition, a chamber where identities soften. I couldn't stop thinking about the person who placed them— how strong their urge must be to create a sense of home inside something that never stops moving.

The Warsaw-Berlin train was late. On such a long journey, extra hours count twice. The main delay occurred earlier in Lviv, where drones bound for Europe were shot down.

While Kyiv feels tense and electric, with golden orange hues shining through metal and tuned to the pitch of imminent danger, Berlin feels, in contrast, porous and sleepy. It's a dimly lit place for reflection. The streets are sparsely illuminated. Its infamous twilight can be seen as the perpetual rehearsal of a blackout.

Back home, my supposed safe space feels peculiar, as if it remembers an old version of me. I took off my pendant and finally fell asleep. The next morning, I woke up to the sound of sirens.

A test alarm. But Berlin's sirens lack the torn note of despair—the depth of urgency, the human cry inside the tone. It doesn't impress me much. I keep wondering if empathy can awaken without the sound of sirens ●

1　K41 (also called ꙥ or Kyrylivska 41) is a nightclub in Podil, Kyiv, Ukraine.

2　Insignia of military and civil authorities, especially Kosaks in Ukraine (15th–18th century).

3　Quote from Underground Resistance: "Transition / Windchime," released: 2000, USA.

4　Aldous Huxley, from *The Doors of Perception*: "We live together, we act on, and react to, one another; but always and in all circumstances we are by ourselves. The martyrs go hand in hand into the arena; they are crucified alone. Embraced, the lovers desperately try to fuse their insulated ecstasies into a single self-transcendence; in vain. By its very nature every embodied spirit is doomed to suffer and enjoy in solitude."

Nastya Vogan is a Ukrainian DJ based in Berlin

Tender is the Night

The night is lined with yellow lantern satin.
The lanterns have replaced old trees, and now
one might think this is their afterlife:
distilling juices of electric currents,
occasionally creaking and gathering together local ants,
throwing themselves against our green window-panes
at full speed, like phosphoric hornets,
and then dropping onto the sills, barely alive.
At night all the bodies tighten up and grow nacre,
so they can hide in their shells, like inside a coffin.
The day resembles shallow water,
with empty seashells in the sand.

Julia Stakhivska, 2015

Julia Stakhivska is a poet, columnist, and children's book author.

The Language Question

Mariana Berezovska

For decades, Russia has used the fact that many Ukrainians speak Russian to claim that we are "the same people." Russia has long used language as a tool to deny Ukrainian identity and justify political domination. I often think how absurd this logic would sound in other multilingual countries like Belgium or Switzerland, where sharing an official language with a neighbouring state has never been used to question whether those countries are "real," or to claim that their citizens need to be rescued. Yet this is precisely the argument that has been weaponized in relation to Ukraine. Whenever the possibility of granting Russian any form of official status in Ukraine emerges, it is immediately used by Russian propagandists as proof that Ukraine "belongs" to Russia.

What's equally simple—and powerful—is to resist this narrative by actually speaking Ukrainian. Our language has always been politicized, but now it carries a new meaning: it's a way to reclaim what's ours, to speak for ourselves from inside the country, not from exile. It's a rare moment in our history when, in the middle of a crisis, we finally have a collective voice that can document and define what's happening— in our own language, not through the voices of others.

Ukrainian was dismissed for centuries by intellectuals of the Russian Empire as the language of peasants—something folkloric, emotional, but not intellectual. Most of the sophisticated Ukrainian works in literature, philosophy, and linguistics that challenged this view were written in secret or in exile. For a long time, our culture survived outside the country, carried by those who were forced to leave.

This, in itself, was not unique. Across Europe, during the rise of nation-states, language became a central battleground: identities were claimed, negotiated, or denied through language, and many emerging nations had to fight for the right to speak and write in their own tongue. But in the Ukrainian case, this struggle was systematic and prolonged. Ukrainian writers and thinkers who insisted on using the language were censored, restricted, or denied the right to publish. Many were pushed to study, work, and publish within the Russian Empire, where institutional support and funding were concentrated—even as Ukrainian cultural autonomy was actively suppressed.

The Russian Empire consistently denied Ukraine the conditions for free cultural and linguistic development. Historically, Ukraine was seen as a space of rebellion and resistance—a territory to be controlled, not allowed to articulate itself independently. This dynamic did not last for decades, but for centuries—and we are still living in the middle of this struggle.

Now, however, we are experiencing a rare and extraordinary moment in Ukrainian history—when this intellectual and creative energy has had space to exist within the country rather than in exile abroad. At the same time, the discussion around language is still full of tension: it's a crack between generations, between regions, between people. Yet so many are switching to Ukrainian—not just speaking it, but beginning to think in it—and I want to explore what this shift means.

There's a part of Russian identity that I carry—not something strong or dominant, because I never really had a connection with my Russian father. But I still have vivid memories of spending summers in Pskov until I was seven. I'd switch to Russian over the summer, and it would take time to switch back to Ukrainian once I was home in Lutsk. The last time I went to Pskov as a child, my mom brought me all the way there— a twenty-four-hour train ride from Lutsk. My Ukrainian grandmother would pick me up at the end of the summer, and I still remember her saying that she wouldn't play with me until I switched back to speaking Ukrainian. She would call me *мале кацапеня.*[1] Soon after, the train stopped running. My mother stopped taking me to see my grandparents.

I remember how my Ukrainian kindergarten teachers reacted when I slipped into Russian after coming back from those trips. One time, we had to name words starting with the letter A. I said *arbuz*—the Russian word for watermelon. They corrected me to *harbuz*, which in Ukrainian means "pumpkin"—but in my head, I thought: no, that's *kavun*—that's the Ukrainian word for watermelon. Even then, I had this kind of linguistic awareness—a feeling that words weren't just words. They carried weight. They came from somewhere. They came with something. Now that I know words like "decolonized thinking" and "intersectionality," I suppose they fit in well here. I didn't know them when I was six.

For most of the twentieth century, a Ukrainian intellectual writing about the Ukrainian language could do so only from exile. The center of our linguistic scholarship—the work that shaped how we understand the history, structure, and philosophy of Ukrainian—was produced abroad, outside the country whose language it defended. Yurii Shevelov is the clearest example. One of the most important Ukrainian linguists, literary critics, and historians of language, he left Kharkiv during the WWII and spent the rest of his life in the United States. All his major works—from *Historical Phonology of the Ukrainian Language,* to his essays on Ukrainian identity—were written far from Ukraine, within a diaspora that was trying to keep the culture alive while the Soviet state suppressed it at home. This was the pattern for generations: Ukrainian intellectual thought survived in New York, Munich, Toronto, but rarely in Kyiv or Kharkiv.

And now, suddenly, we are living in a moment when Ukrainian can be written, developed, theorized, and enriched *inside* the country. When people writing in Ukrainian are writing from Kyiv, Lviv, Kharkiv, Odesa—not from exile. It feels like the first time in our modern history that we are not only preserving the language, but expanding it from within. This is something we need to protect and cherish, because it is fragile and unprecedented—a chance that earlier generations of Ukrainian thinkers simply did not have.

In the early 2010s, I studied linguistics at the National Linguistic University in Kyiv. Many of my classmates were from Western Ukraine—not the big cities like Lviv or Ivano-Frankivsk, but small towns and villages. I saw how many of them carried this kind of inferiority complex. As soon as they arrived in Kyiv and went outside of our dorm, especially if they got a student job somewhere, they switched to Russian. There was pressure—real, structural pressure. If you didn't switch, you risked being seen as *selo*, a village person. I never switched, but I could feel it—in public transportation, in shops, asking for directions on the street.

In my first year, we had a professor of "Business Ukrainian," a renowned linguist—at that time, she was even teaching Yulia Tymoshenko to speak Ukrainian (so many memes pop into my head as I write this). At one of our first classes, she said, in this snobbish tone: "Here we don't say *тудою сюдою*.[2] That's what you say in the village you came from."

I was absolutely shocked to discover that these words were "forbidden." They were *so* useful—the Ukrainian equivalents of the English *hereby/thereby*,

The Language Question

or German *hier lang/dort lang.* I couldn't grasp how such useful words could be bullied out of standard language.

I remember coming back to my hometown and forcing my mom also to stop using those words, not to sound like *selo*, and to say *цією дорогою, цим шляхом*[3] instead. Much later, when I was doing my Master's in linguistics in Potsdam, I wrote my thesis on "the prestige of a language"—why some languages and accents become "prestigious" while others don't. Outlining how we form impressions of people simply based on the way they speak, often reading authority, intelligence, or cultural value into an accent—even though language tells us nothing about a person's character or abilities.

This phenomenon has been widely studied in the context of British English—its colonial history, the suppression of local languages, and the internal hierarchy of accents within Britain itself. It has long been understood how English, and particularly its more prestigious accents, came to dominate places that historically had their own languages but were denied the conditions to develop them fully or take pride in their distinct linguistic traditions. Thanks to Kneecap,[4] this discussion became newly visible and widely renewed in 2025.

My thesis focused on the lack of prestige in Ukrainian, as compared to Russian, in big cities, and its historical context—how major cities were formed around industries, how books became published mainly in Russian, how standard use of Russian in the education system spread, and how spoken Ukrainian became reduced to the language of "village people." For example, very few people know that even in Donbas, most villages are still Ukrainian-speaking—it's the cities that are Russian-speaking. I even included *тудою/сюдою*[5] in my thesis, but couldn't find enough scholarly evidence explaining why these instrumental words never became part of standard Ukrainian.

The language question was always there. I always tied it back to why I never fully integrated into Kyiv, back in the 2010s—why I never really felt at home there. Funnily enough, now that I've returned from Berlin to Kyiv to live here again in 2025, I've ended up in the same neighbourhood where my student dorm used to be. The area has changed a lot—new modern residential complexes everywhere—but the vibe is still the same.

Surprisingly, I hear a lot of Ukrainian in the shops and the metro, and on the streets. Mostly Ukrainian, actually. Many teenagers still speak Russian, though. In front of the district hall and the local gymnasium, there is a large memorial to the people from this area who have been killed in the war since 2022—their stories are written there. I wish that the school kids walking past this memorial could understand how much speaking Ukrainian can mean—not as an obligation, but as a way of acknowledging what this war is being fought for, and of honoring the people who gave their lives so that they can go to school, grow up, and live in a free Ukraine.

I also think about those who were tortured and killed in Russian captivity, where speaking Ukrainian was forbidden—precisely because their captors could not understand it. In their lives, language was not abstract. It is something people were punished for, and something they held on to even then.

Yet still, some people speak as if they've been evacuated from Moscow. I find this really sad, because I understand that not everyone is living through this war equally. I find it very, very sad—especially when it comes to the new generation who is supposed to keep living in a liberated Ukraine.

During my first years at university, when I could finally travel alone, I went back to Russia twice to visit my grandmother after eleven years without seeing her. The last time I was there, I remember waiting for my train to Kyiv at a station in the Pskov region, called Stantsiya Dno. *Dno* means "bottom," as in "rock bottom."[6]

I was sitting on a bench for a few hours, reading *Dictionary of the Khazars: A Lexicon Novel.*[7] A drunk guy sat down next to me, commented on the book because he somehow knew Milorad Pavić, his phone rang, its ringtone a song from the band Muse, and then he was picked up by *менти*.[8] I wanted to use the bathroom but the door wouldn't lock, so I just stayed on the bench until my train arrived.

In my mind, Russia is this station. It is *dno*. It is *менти*. It is drunk guys, a vague longing for culture, and eternal suffering. I sometimes wish everyone who still speaks Russian could visit Stantsiya Dno—to see what it means to be in Russia, and how lucky they are not to be there.

In my school years in Lutsk, I studied violin for seven years. My violin teacher, Igor Smetanin, and his wife, a pianist, were respected intellectuals in town and spoke Russian. Their family must have come to Lutsk because of military dislocation (someone in the family, probably his father, had been in the military and was stationed there). Like all the other Russian families you'd come across, they never switched to Ukrainian. They always spoke Russian—with this subtle but constant distance. Like: *we are not the same as you*. It was never aggressive, but always present—this undercurrent of separateness.

My mom would always switch to Russian when speaking with them. She was nostalgic for her years studying in Russia and the "greatness of Russian literature." It always irritated me. I'd think: *respect yourself, Mom. Don't do that*. And I just kept speaking Ukrainian.

Their son, Illia Smetanin, was my age, and studied violin at the same time. He moved on to the conservatory, and became an acclaimed violinist. Their family always had this aura—refined, educated, above the provincial. The intellectual elite of the town.

When the full-scale invasion started in 2022, it turned out that Illia was a traitor. He had been recruited by Russia before 2014, when he had travelled to Moscow, apparently as one of those people they claimed needed "saving" from Western Ukraine. He ended up working for the Russian army. He was involved in blowing up the military landing airport in my hometown.

Now, after the invasion, many of my friends in Kyiv have switched to Ukrainian. What surprised me most was how effortlessly it happened—how natural they suddenly sounded. My closest friends here are from Kyiv and the surrounding towns, from Donetsk and Luhansk, Kharkiv, and the Dnipropetrovsk region— all hardcore Russian speakers before. The ease of this shift genuinely shocked me.

I know that some of them had difficulties switching their thinking and reading habits. Some still experience tension with their parents, who continue speaking Russian. That being said, it's essential to understand that the generations have changed radically, and there is no point trying to change those who are nostalgic for the Soviet Union, for their youth, for the aspirations of that time. The future belongs to the people who are fighting this war and who will survive it. Many of us won't.

For Ukrainians abroad who still speak Russian, I have only one question: how are you not ashamed to be mistaken for a Russian?

                                        The Language Question

I know very well that there are many different opinions on this—even some of the contributors to this book are Russian speakers, and I've honestly questioned whether I even want to be in the same book as them. When this thought crosses my mind, I recognize how snobbish it is, and that I don't know their story. One day, I want to interview more people who still speak Russian—to better understand their logic, or at least to document this phenomenon.

I also know that I'm in this privileged position, sitting on a high (Ukrainian) horse, judging those below who struggle to speak Ukrainian. I come from the west; I had great teachers; my family always spoke Ukrainian and never watched Solovyov.[9] My uncle's garage door is painted in black and red.[10] I am, frankly, a perfect profile for Russian propaganda to justify the invasion and its so-called "liberation": someone who can be presented as an "evil Nazi" figure, supposedly making the lives of Russian speakers in Ukraine intolerable, denying them the right to exist freely, and thus reinforcing the claim that Russian speakers need to be "liberated" from Ukrainians like me.

But I also carry stories that complicate this picture—and they matter to me. Stories of friends who moved from occupied Crimea and Donbas to Kyiv or abroad, and had to rethink who they are. Stories of following Russian propaganda for years, and then slowly unlearning it—not through slogans or school textbooks rewritten with every change of government, but through personal encounters and lived experience. Stories of people who switched to Ukrainian and can no longer find common ground with their parents. Of mixed families, of Soviet-era migrations, of identities formed by circumstances rather than choice. Of people who resist

switching languages not out of loyalty to Russia, but
out of distrust toward the Ukrainian state, or a feeling
of having been abandoned by it. Stories of minorities
in Ukraine, whose cultures and languages have also not
been sufficiently heard or protected.

Ukraine is large and deeply complex—a country of
more than forty million people before the full-scale
invasion, shaped by centuries of violent, exploitative,
and rebellious history that long predates Russia's
appearance as an imperial power—and no single story
can contain it.[11]

And yet, beyond all these personal stories, and
beyond the complexity of identities—people's histories,
the places they come from, what they speak and how—
there is one thing I carry that feels simple and absolute,
even when everything else is layered and messy. What
guides me in this war—the one that takes place as
I write—is the voice of Kateryna Motrych, the actress
and wife of Ukrainian actor and soldier, Yuriy Felipenko,
who was killed in the war in early 2025. At his funeral,
standing over his body, her voice breaking, she said:

"I want to ask everyone—kill everything Russian in
yourself. It's because of Russia that we're here today,
looking at Yuriy's cold body. Forget the language of
the enemy. Take revenge."

Whatever it takes—*you have to kill the Russia in
yourself to survive this war.* For me, language is one of
the most powerful ways to do that. It's the clearest
way to say where I stand ●

Mariana Berezovska is a writer, curator, and cultural producer working
between Berlin and Kyiv. She is the co-founder of the magazine *Borshch*
and label manager at Standard Deviation.

                                        The Language Question

1   Literally "little katsap." *Katsap* is a derogatory Ukrainian word for
    a Russian, and adding *мале* ("little") turns it into something that sounds
    almost cute or teasing, even though the meaning isn't soft at all.

2   *Tudoyu* [tuˈdoju] and *syudoyu* [sʲuˈdoju] are historically native Ukrainian
    words recorded in dictionaries. In contemporary Ukrainian they
    are considered colloquial or dialectal, which is why they were avoided
    in the official standard, although the words themselves remain
    completely natural and useful.

3   Translates to "by going this way."

4   Kneecap is an Irish hip-hop trio from Belfast, Northern Ireland.
    The group advocates for the legal status and revitalization of the Irish
    language (Gaeilge) in Northern Ireland, a cause that has deep roots
    in a shared history of anti-colonial resistance and the sociopolitical
    context of the post-Troubles era.

5   Ibid., footnote 2.

6   Translates as "bottom" in both Ukrainian and Russian.

7   *Dictionary of the Khazars: A Lexicon Novel* (Serbian Cyrillic: Хазарски
    речник, Hazarski rečnik) is the first novel by Serbian writer Milorad
    Pavić, published in 1984. I read it as part of my university studies.

8   "Мєнти" is a Russian slang word for police. In this context,
    it is deliberately written in Ukrainian spelling.

9   Vladimir Solovyov is a Russian journalist and television presenter,
    best known as the host of the political talk shows *Evening with Vladimir
    Solovyov* and *Moscow. Kremlin. Putin* on the state-owned channel
    Russia-1, as well as *Solovyov Live*. He is a prominent figure in Kremlin
    state media and an outspoken supporter of Russia's war against
    Ukraine, the annexation of Crimea, and Vladimir Putin's policies.

10 Red and black are the colors of the flag of the Ukrainian Insurgent
    Army (UPA), which is associated with the Ukrainian liberation
    movement of the twentieth century. The colors are commonly inter-
    preted as symbolizing blood shed for liberation and land.

11 For those interested in understanding the broader historical context
    of modern Ukraine and its relationships with neighbouring empires,
    I personally recommend the lecture series *The Making of Modern
    Ukraine* by Timothy Snyder (Yale Courses, YouTube).

Flicker

It seems to me that this is what hell might look like—
a gleaming structure of glass and metal: a few levels
	up, several rings down.
Everyone is rushing around, bored and tense with
	anticipation.
Eurydice's train has arrived, Persephone rides up
	the escalator,
Charon in his wetsuit turns his oar.
But above all—there are too many of them—it's a full
	moon, excess, noise.
Maneuvers on the wings of the firebird. The flame
	thaws on my tongue.
I escape this whirlwind, run into the cool of the night,
	to the lake,
kiss the wall of the house above it.
Who said that what is real must always bang?
	The thunderstorm?
Slowly I walk along the canal of the street.
The sky is full of stars today!
On the western front, they put on
the most spectacular show.
Somewhere in the north, a gray Kynokephale rales in
	its dusty corridors.
A star shows him the way to Tartarus.
Slowly, slowly, the moon's little ship sets sail
to take him to—but no, that won't happen either—
Riddled with holes, hit by the splinter of my country.
The moral law within us flickers.

Julia Stakhivska, 2023

Not Ready for the Light

Yuliia Leites

Every time before he was wounded, he dreamt it. The night before the 152-millimeter shell struck his position, R dreamed again:

He was back in his grandmother's summer garden— the place of childhood safety, lilac bushes, and rusted swings. There stood a guardian gnome, one of those small painted figures that usually guard nothing.

In the dream the gnome started talking to him and pointed toward a freshly dug grave. When R looked closer, the grave had no bottom—it opened into a black hole. The gnome told him to jump in. R refused. "Not today," he said. "I have things to do. You can wait."

The next morning the shell hit the bunker directly. The blast caved in the roof, buried him alive under logs and soil. His comrade, by some act of impossible intuition, dug him out before he suffocated. His spine crushed, his body splintered by the wooden beams of the blindage.

He was evacuated to a field hospital, then to the central. Morphine entered his blood—at first as medicine, then as promise. Like Marianne Faithfull's song "Sister Morphine," the line between healing and disappearance blurred.

Later, when he told me this dream, I heard it not as prophecy but as the psyche's rehearsal of annihilation. Dreams like these visit many soldiers: anticipatory phantasies that stage death in the space of sleep, so the waking body can keep moving. The unconscious, unable to prevent the incoming shell, tries instead to represent it—to contain what cannot be contained.

In psychoanalytic language, sleeping and dreaming are two different processes. Sleeping is the nightly work of keeping the psyche intact re-charging the body. Dreaming, as Freud describes it, is a psychic function that protects sleep from desires and fears which are almost never at rest, those which try to wake us up, interrupting the charging process. So the psyche comes up with a solution in the form of dream-work—constant symbolisation of the raw material of the unconscious into images, stories, fragments of meaning. Thus the gnome performs the role of a psychopomp—a figure of transition—marking the moment when the dream-work protects sleep-work—metabolizing terror when the body cannot rest.

The dream above was shared with me by a client—a soldier of the Armed Forces of Ukraine—with whom I began psychoanalytic psychotherapy in early 2023.

A year and a half into our work, R brought another dream.

> *He was sitting among the ruins of a* mikrorayon—*one of those Soviet-era residential suburbs made of identical panel buildings arranged around a small communal courtyard. In the middle stood a children's playground: a sandpit, a bent slide, the skeleton of a swing. It was somewhere in the east of Ukraine—one of those cities you only hear about in the news, somewhere near the frontline.*

It was where a generation, raised under an empire disguised as communism, first learned what "we" meant. The "we" now fractured into the we who are still there and the we who left.

In his dream R was sitting on a bench in a children's playground, surrounded by half-destroyed apartment blocks. Everything was in black and white, silent, devoid of life.

He suddenly felt the need to call me. He reached for his phone, which was in the right pocket of his pants. But when he tried to pull it out, he realized that all five fingers on his hand were broken. They were there, but they would not respond— as if they no longer obeyed him. The darkness around him thickened as he tried desperately to dial my number.

Then, all at once, a thin line of light appeared— a clear, horizontal incision. He felt compelled to cross it. On the other side was Khreshchatyk Street in central Kyiv, flooded with sun and color, a day of celebration: families walking, women with flowers, children laughing.

While standing there, he looked down and saw his clothes—filthy, stiff from blood and earth from the trenches. The smell of smoke and decay clung to him. The light around him was blinding, almost accusatory. He understood that he didn't belong to this brightness, it exposed rather than welcomed him. And then he felt it—the gravity of the dark, familiar, heavy—pulling him back toward it.

He made his choice and stepped back into the dark, finding himself once more at the ruined playground, trying again, with his broken fingers, to dial my number.

That's when he woke up.

When R told me this dream, I kept returning to the place itself. The playground in the center of a *mikrorajon*—ringed by those uniform Soviet panel blocks—was once part of an architecture of belonging, an image that united generations.

Now, in his dream, that space appears in monochrome: no light, no color, only gradations of ash. The collective space has survived, but only as a photographic negative of itself, remaining in the darkroom of the psyche, still wet, still trembling, not yet ready to be developed. Not ready for the light.

For me, such rejection of light is not a negative regression but preservation. The psyche withdraws from exposure the way a wound closes against air—the temporary darkness is needed to keep healing possible.

This is what I see, again and again, in those who cannot sleep, or who cannot wake fully, or who have left—not an avoidance of life, but a strange kind of loyalty to it. Some part of the organism knows it has to pull back before carrying on.

In the 1970's, two Chilean biologists, Humberto Maturana and Francisco Varela, offered a language for this movement. They called it autopoiesis—from the Greek *auto*, self, and *poiein*, to make. A living system, they wrote, exists not because of the matter that composes it but because of the continuous work through which it repairs itself. A cell stays alive only by renewing the membrane that separates it from what might dissolve it.

But this logic of self-making belongs not only to cells. Rivers live by it too. They withdraw from their own banks, erode them, redraw them—always producing the shape that keeps them alive. When the current becomes too strong, the river folds, pulls inward, digs a new path through silt and shadow. It does not abandon its course; it remakes it. I often think the psyche works the same way. When the environment turns toxic, it retreats just enough to continue its flow.

Both sleeping and leaving are, in their own ways, small and large versions of the same movement—allowing the regeneration of the self, a temporary retreat that makes survival possible.

When sleep fails—as it so often does in war—the mental system stays open to the bombardment, both literal and psychic, until it begins to collapse. That is what I see in the dreams of soldiers—not prophecy, not mysticism, but a desperate maintenance of being, an invisible repair that happens in the dark, where the psyche rehearses its own demise.

Leaving follows a similar logic, only on another scale. It is not exile in the classical or tragic sense, not 'nostos'—the longing to return home—but something closer to a macro-sleep. It is the psyche's way of dimming the light when the exposure to reality grows unbearable. Those who leave Ukraine, or any place of catastrophe, do not step away from belonging, but from both physical and psychic annihilation. To depart is just another way to preserve the ability to feel.

Sleep, leaving, silence are the pauses through which reality becomes thinkable again. They are the psyche's slow acts of autopoiesis, the work of re-creating a boundary, of saying softly: I am still here, even if for now I must stay in the dark.

At the same time, every drone video, every televised frontline, every ruined building demands to be seen. But psychic life works differently, it cannot survive while constantly exposed. It needs opacity, latency, and the off-frame. It might seem as the rage against the light, the negation of truth, I see it as hibernation, the condition for meaning to return.

Even in the dark, memory continues to develop.
One just needs to find a way to wake, to dream, to keep
dialing a number ●

Yuliia Leites is a psychoanalytic psychotherapist from Kyiv, Ukraine,
and a candidate at the International Psychoanalytical Association through
the Ukrainian Study Group.

 Not Ready for the Light

Notes from a Third Space

Ніхто

In 2018, I moved to Kyiv to help create what I hoped
would become a "third space"—a place beyond the
binaries of nationality, gender, and the hierarchies that
shape much of our social worlds. A space of freedom
where these values could be lived, not merely discussed.
For five years, I worked to co-create this space, alongside Ukrainian colleagues, for Ukrainian audiences,
in a Ukrainian city that was itself trying to define what
"Ukrainian" meant in the first place.

This text is written from that position: deeply
involved but perpetually outside, committed to what
we were building, which was both celebrated as
a symbol of a "new Ukraine," and criticized as being
"not from here." Welcomed for bringing international
connections and yet met with suspicion for being the
outsider who brought them. I've lived between Berlin
and Kyiv, between languages, between the assumption
that I belonged nowhere, and between the daily work
of creating a place where others could belong.

I write semi-anonymously, as Ніхто—no one, nobody—not to evade responsibility for these observations, but because the story isn't mine alone: it involves
colleagues and friends I won't name, dynamics I can
only describe in aggregate, a project I still care deeply
to protect, even while questioning some of what happened within and around it. I write from the invitation
to contribute to this publication, which has asked
for a perspective from someone positioned *between*—
inside enough to have seen, outside enough to have
been marked as outside. This is not a claim to objectivity;
it's a specific vantage point with specific blindnesses—
and specific lines of sight.

I'm aware that what follows is shaped by my own
experience—an experience that, whatever it's meant to

me, remains small against what Ukrainians face daily.
I've tried to separate what I've observed from what
I felt, but I can't fully succeed. What I can do is be hon-
est about the entanglement, and write from a position
of solidarity with Ukraine's struggle for survival and
sovereignty—not despite the critiques that follow, but
because of them.

Foundation

I struggled for years to understand why the assertion
came so quickly, so reflexively, from certain colleagues—
people I thought of as like-minded, roughly my age—
this insistence that I would never understand Kyiv, that
I didn't come from here, that my presence was simultaneously necessary (because we needed "European
standards," "international connections," "world-class
expertise") and illegitimate (because how dare an
outsider presume to shape what should be authentically
Ukrainian). It wasn't everyone, of course—there were
many who approached the work differently, who saw
collaboration as something other than a zero-sum
game of authenticity. However, the pattern was consistent enough, vocal enough, to structure how decisions
were made, what could be said, and who could speak
without the preface of, "but of course, you're not
from here."

It took me longer than it should have to recognize
what was perhaps obvious: that this wasn't really about
me at all. The people who articulated this most clearly
weren't outside critics—they were colleagues in posi-
tions of real influence who helped build what we built.
And yet something remained unresolved—as if the
project could be fully theirs only by not being partly
mine. Perhaps they were right. Perhaps I did represent

                            Notes from a Third Space

an asymmetry of resources and recognition that repro-
duced exactly the hierarchies we claimed to be disman-
tling. Perhaps there were histories at work that I had
no access to, I couldn't know for certain. But being
marked as outside was also a position from which certain mechanisms became visible: how the question of
belonging operated, what work it did, who got to ask it
and who had to answer. I stood at the edge where usually unspoken rules had to be articulated, often against
me. I could not control how my presence was read;
what I could do was pay attention to the reading itself.

However, to reduce those five years to that single
dynamic would mean to erase what actually sustained
the project: the thousands of people—young Ukrainians,
mostly, but not only—who came every weekend,
queued for hours in winter, traveled from other cities.
They understood, immediately and viscerally, what
kind of space this was trying to be. These were people
who had been waiting for exactly this: a sex-positive,
queer-friendly space where cameras were banned and
judgments left at the door. Where you could dance
without performing. Where all of this was simply lived,
not debated—made real in the bodies moving on the
dance floor and the care structures we built to hold
them. There was an openness in these crowds, a hunger
for connection across boundaries—linguistic, national,
sexual—that felt genuinely curious about difference,
eager to encounter the unfamiliar. Perhaps this had to
do with the space being new, hard-won, not yet taken
for granted. In Kyiv, this openness felt urgent, careful
and alive—a feeling I hope will never be lost.

The club had become a node in a network of like-
minded spaces. And this, I think, is what gets lost in
the debates about authenticity and outside influence:

that the space worked not because it imposed something external, but because it resonated with something
already present—a desire that existed in Kyiv long
before we arrived, a desire for exactly this kind of
freedom, this kind of openness, this kind of world. We
didn't create that desire; we just built a structure for
it. Over five years, I had perhaps a thousand conversations with people who came—at the bar, in the smoking
area, waiting in line. The question of authenticity never
came up. Not once. They simply claimed the space,
made it real through being there. The authenticity
discourse emerged elsewhere, from cultural journalists
and self-appointed arbiters—and I began to wonder
what function it actually served.

Threshold

What had been a productive tension—building something together across differences—had hardened to
an impasse: was this space authentically Ukrainian,
or was my involvement proof that it couldn't be?
I found myself increasingly caught in conversations
that assumed these were the only options.

I remember a conversation on Trukhaniv Island
with a friend—someone I respected, open-minded
and internationally oriented—explaining to me with
a certain careful patience that, *of course* the club was
important, *of course* it represented something vital,
but didn't I see the problem...the optics, that a *foreigner*
had been part of creating the space? What did that
say about Ukraine, about Ukrainians, about their capacity to shape their own modernity—as if my presence
were evidence that they couldn't.

I'd learned quickly that asking questions made
things worse—as they could be read as a defensiveness,

                                    Notes from a Third Space

a refusal to listen. But I'd wanted to ask: where exactly had these values come from? Why was queerness considered Western—what about queer people in Kyiv who'd been there all along? Had the desire for spaces without hierarchies been merely imported—what about those who'd organized underground parties for years? Was the hunger for freedom something we brought or something we simply recognized, resonated with, built a structure around?

I understood the pain in that statement, could hear in it a history I hadn't experienced—and I began to realize that this wasn't a tension that time or shared work would resolve. The ambivalence had always been there; what was new was my growing certainty that it always would be. What stayed with me, though, was why: how easily the word "foreigner" came, even from colleagues who would have rejected cruder nationalism—used as though merely descriptive, without seeming to notice that the designation itself was already doing a kind of work: separating, categorizing, determining who could speak as insider and who would carry an asterisk. The vocabulary may have been softer, but I wondered whether the logic underneath was any different than any of us wanted to believe.

Shadows

By 2021, the question of who belonged was making itself felt differently—gradually, the way winter arrives in Kyiv. There had always been resistance: predictable conservative outrage about queerness and drugs. And now something harder: organized groups that didn't bother with discourse or debate, but showed up with balaclavas and smoke bombs. Even they framed their violence as protecting 'real' Ukrainian values against

Western degeneracy—positioning queer spaces as foreign impositions, queer people as fundamentally alien to Ukrainian-ness itself. I remember the first time someone threw a bottle at the entrance, how we almost laughed about it, treated it like random hooliganism, not yet understanding that this was testing our defenses, seeing how we would respond, whether anyone would protect us. The police certainly wouldn't—they had made that clear enough through their own harassment, the random drug searches, the way they would position their cars just close enough to intimidate, but far enough away to claim they weren't interfering.

By November 2021, the weekend disruptions had become almost routine—every Saturday throughout the autumn, the same groups showing up, the same balaclavas, the same police standing nearby, smoking, watching, carefully not intervening in the occasional throwing of stones and flares across the walls of the old factory. By late autumn, the Telegram channels were explicit: lists of clubs to shut down, photographs of "degenerates" to identify, calls for action against those who were "corrupting Ukrainian youth." What made the club's anniversary different was its scale: international DJs, over a thousand people waiting in the cold—while thirty masked men blocked the entrance and fifteen officers stood nearby. For ninety minutes a mediator negotiated; the police kept insisting we were causing the disturbance. Eventually the pressure of a thousand people in freezing temperatures became untenable, and the gate was opened. But what stayed with me was the image of those officers, watching young and queer people being threatened week after week, doing nothing, insisting the problem was us, silently agreeing with the attackers.

Later we learned what everyone suspected: the blockades were paid for by a rival developer, and these financial interests intersected with the ideological goals of far-right networks around Yevhen Karas—a figure whose networks had been involved in attacks on queer-friendly spaces across Kyiv. After the invasion, reports suggested something more unsettling: that some far-right movements operating before 2022 may have been infiltrated, or supported through Russian influence campaigns. But at that moment I just felt exhausted, as if we were fighting a battle we had already lost—not because they were stronger, but because they had never had to play by any rules at all.

Inversion

February 24, 2022. The full-scale invasion changed everything—but it's worth lingering on how it reordered who could be criticized, and what questions could be asked.

The men who had targeted us—the networks around Karas—were now at the front. Many fighting. Some dying. Whatever one thought about their politics, they were putting their bodies between the invasion and the city. That fact reordered all other considerations, made previous critiques feel petty—the complaints of people who had the luxury of caring about homophobia when tanks rolled toward the capital. I felt it myself: the vertigo of watching gratitude and critique become impossible to hold simultaneously, of watching questions become unspeakable—not because they were answered—but because the war made asking them seem like betrayal.

But the invasion didn't only rehabilitate those who had attacked us; it also illuminated something I had observed since 2018: a casualness among young people about certain fascist symbols—the Black Sun tattooed on someone's calf, the Wolfsangel on a patch. The cultural gatekeepers who had so much to say about authenticity had remarkably little to say about this. The Black Sun was designed by Heinrich Himmler's occultists; it has no other history, and yet the conversation never seemed to happen.

Now, some of those who had worn these symbols were fighting at the front, becoming heroes. I watched as fundraising campaigns in the West couldn't support certain units—the Azov battalion defending Mariupol, in fighting so brutally, had become a symbol of Ukrainian resistance—but they still carried the Black Sun in their insignia. Having been shaped by a German context in which these symbols are unambiguous and unspeakable, I carry a specific relationship to them that makes certain things impossible to unsee—and probably obscures others. And yet: I never found a way to raise these questions publicly, never risked the accusation of imposing German frameworks onto a context I didn't fully understand. In this sense, I participated in the very silence I am now describing. What stayed with me was the structure of that silence—not disagreement, not a different interpretation I could engage with, but the sense that raising the question at all marked you as someone imposing foreign frameworks onto a context where they didn't apply. Before the invasion, during the invasion, this deflection remained the same. I worry about what gets normalized in such silence, including my own.

Walls

By 2023, something had shifted—not just in how my involvement was understood, but in how belonging

Notes from a Third Space

itself was being negotiated across Ukrainian society. New fractures were emerging even as the war
demanded solidarity. I watched these fault lines form
in conversations, in group chats, in the small moments
where someone was made to feel they hadn't done
enough, hadn't stayed long enough, hadn't sacrificed in the right way. Those who stayed versus those
who left. Those who fought versus those who hid
from conscription.

The boundaries were turning inward, Ukrainian
against Ukrainian—and outward, toward anyone
marked as foreign. I remember when Macron called
Putin early in the invasion, and word went around to
'cancel all French people'—as if an entire nation could
be reduced to its president's phone call. International
collaborations were quietly discontinued. Artists who
had played regularly stopped being invited. Colleagues
found their messages unanswered, their involvement
reframed as no longer necessary.

There was a pattern I recognized, though I suspect it extended far beyond my experience: a kind
of circularity where conditions for participation are
gradually removed, and then the resulting absence
becomes evidence of insufficient commitment.
Reduced presence becomes proof of inadequate
dedication, justifying further distance, confirming the
original suspicion. Whether intentional or simply how
things unfold, perhaps it doesn't matter. Standing at
the boundary made this pattern visible to me precisely
because I was the object of the reframing: I watched
years of collaboration become rewritten remarkably
quickly, not erased exactly, but backgrounded, made
to seem less central than they had been. Those doing
the reframing may have experienced it as natural

clarification, a necessary adjustment to new realities. From where I stood, it looked like a mechanism that, once set in motion, would not stop with people like me.

What concerns me is what happens when this logic extends beyond the emergency—when the networks that connected Ukraine to the world are allowed to atrophy, when openness itself becomes suspect. The relationships that took years to build can be severed in months. Rebuilding them will be harder.

Fragments

Whatever my own experience of gradual exclusion meant, it remained small against what others faced. The fractures ran through everyone differently. A woman from Kherson who had spent months doing volunteer work during the occupation—Russian-speaking because that was the language she grew up with—returned to Kyiv and found herself met with suspicion, with corrections, with a coldness that said: your Russian marks you as not quite Ukrainian enough, even though you helped and never left. For those who had never been granted full belonging in the first place—queer people, minorities, those who didn't fit the emerging national narrative—the ground was even less stable.

Since the invasion, queer Ukrainians have organized in ways that should have made their belonging undeniable: forming their own units within the army, building NGOs to support LGBT+ soldiers at the front, doing the work of survival and resistance simultaneously. Many had done everything that should have mattered—fought, volunteered, organized mutual aid. And yet whether they stayed or left, the bind only tightened:

stay, and face a future where the men who hunted you before the war return as armed heroes, untouchable; leave, and lose everything—friends, the right to return, the belonging you spent years insisting on.

A friend who had been part of the scene from the beginning—openly queer, someone who had spent years fighting for his right to exist in Kyiv—worked with military units after the invasion, fighting discrimination from within. For years he stayed, insisted on belonging until one day he decided he couldn't anymore. He fled via the green border to the EU, risking detention, risking everything. The cost was immediate: friends stopped contact, and now he cannot return home for who knows how many years, as he moves from country to country throughout Europe. "I spent years proving I belonged," he told me. "At some point I realized: I shouldn't have to prove anything."

In Summer 2025, someone connected to the networks around Karas—the same groups that had attacked us in 2021—showed up at the door with a weapon, threatened security, and demanded entry. The incident was never reported. Not because it wasn't serious, but because reporting it would mean accusing someone who had fought at the front, and in the current climate, that felt like betraying the army itself. This is what concerns me most: not that violence happens, but that certain violence has become unreportable. The groups that targeted queer spaces before the war are armed now, officially, with the status that comes from having fought. The question isn't whether they'll use this power—they're already using it. The question is what happens when certain people become untouchable, when the status of defender extends to those whose targets haven't changed.

Horizons

Third spaces aren't secondary, and aren't things you add after the 'real work' is done. They're where the society that's being fought for actually takes form, in miniature. The thousands who come to the club every weekend aren't escaping reality; they are creating it—and the fact that this happens at night, with music and dancing, doesn't make it less politically significant than the daytime work of legislation and policy. If anything, it's more foundational, because it's where people experience, viscerally and collectively, what it feels like to live in a society organized around principles other than domination and control. Once you've felt that, you can't forget it.

These freedoms, however, are not guaranteed. The question of how to deal with the groups and symbols and ideologies that have helped save the country, yet threaten the freedoms this country claims to be fighting for—can't be avoided forever, can't be postponed until some imagined post-war moment when nuance feels affordable. It's happening now, in the ways we talk about who fought, and what they fought for, in the ways certain symbols get normalized and certain critiques get foreclosed.

Yet, here is what gets lost in the discourse of survival: Ukraine is fighting for something, not just against something. For freedom—existing without fear, without having to justify your presence. For democracy—where dissent is possible without being labeled betrayal. For self-determination—the right to participate in shaping what 'we' means. These values cannot be defended in theory while violated in practice. Third spaces are where they become real.

Shaping that future will require all Ukrainians—those who stayed and those who left, those who fought and those who contributed otherwise, those who fit emerging narratives and those who never did. It will require rethinking collaboration as strength, critique as care. And something harder still: a willingness to sit with discomfort, to resist resolving every tension by determining who belongs and who doesn't. Third spaces proved this is viable: that strength comes from openness, that a society can be fiercely protective of its sovereignty while remaining genuinely open to difference.

That capacity—the openness I saw in those crowds, the genuine curiosity about difference—it still exists, battered but functioning. Whether it survives what comes next will be determined by Ukrainians, through thousands of small decisions about whose voices matter, which spaces deserve protection, what kind of society this was all for. Ukraine's future will be determined not by who can claim the most authentic connection to its past, but by who shows up to build that future. I can only say I saw that it was possible. And I hope that's worth something, even coming from someone who, in the end, turned out to be no one after all ●

Hixto arrived in Kyiv in 2018 to work on a space that does not exist. Hixto means "nobody."

Ghosts

Still the same landscape, but the undertones of the
      chill are slightly bluish.
Morning mists are getting more and more challenging.
Steel hawks take off—we can't see them, these
      fighter jets,
but they are there, behind the clouds. Like ghosts.
And below, the same comely sky—alpine meadows
      with lamb-like clouds,
and the wind, a cold shepherd, forms a flock out
      of them.
Not that we are scared, not at all.
On somebody's windowsill, a watermelon displays
      its green eye.
Your mother plays Bach. The tireless churchgoer…
Only at night does somebody eat the heart with
      a tiny spoon
that clinks as it touches the plate's bottom.

Julia Stakhivska, 2015

On Blood and the Most Radical Gesture of Care

62

Notes on Art During Wartime

Oksana Briukhovetska

"When there is an open wound on the body, initially, it bleeds or rots. It gets treated and is gradually healing, getting covered with a crust of dried blood." These words accompanied the project by Ukrainian artist Yuliia Danylevska, who, at the beginning of the full-scale Russian invasion of Ukraine, lived for some time in occupied Kherson. Yuliia's work, based on interviews with neurodivergent female artists conducted in 2025, is titled "The Wound Thawed Like Ice." She spoke with these artists about how neurodiversity affects their practices—not only creativity, but also through cooperation with institutions, and the ability to meet the requirements of the artistic world. Yuliia states to have carried out this project in an attempt to overcome her own psychological crisis. The artist's gesture is as follows: when you are struggling, you turn to those who are also suffering—perhaps even more than you. This gesture goes beyond art; it is rather a gesture of care, caused by one's own suffering. These conversations revealed that it is not only neurodivergence that creates barriers. Barriers are often established by the premises on which the art world is built, such as competitiveness, hierarchy, focus on productivity and success. In my preface to the book[1] where the project is published, I wrote:

> *Yuliia's small survey is significant in a much broader context, too. Mental disorders are not always inherited and lifelong. Psychological problems and emotional breakdowns can materialize at any stage of life, triggered by external stressors. In Ukraine, a country which has been at war for eleven years now, a huge number of people are in need of help and support. We need to build our society on completely different foundations. It shouldn't just be*

When I say that the project goes beyond art,
it means that it becomes a public practice of care.
However, later it returns to art in the form of an artistic work or text. A crust of dried blood protecting
the wound and providing it with the opportunity to
heal is a metaphor for how art can work when there is
a need to overcome a personal psychological crisis.
Such practices already exist in Ukrainian society and
art today, often outside institutions and without any
formal funding. They are becoming closely aligned
with the volunteer practices and fundraising efforts for
the Ukrainian military that have become widespread
during the full-scale war.

Reflecting on caring and going beyond art, I am
faced with the question: Isn't the decision to go to the
front to fight—which in our case means to defend—
the most radical gesture of public care in our war-torn
times? Some artists resorted to this most radical of gestures: they decided to fight for Ukraine. Some of those
defenders were killed in action. The deaths of artists,
such as that of queer artist and musician Arthur Snitkus
in 2024, Marharyta Polovinko and Davyd Chychkan
in 2025, are traumatic events that bring the artistic
community together in grieving. These deaths also
represent ruptures of the artistic bubble, connecting to
a broader community of people who've joined the fight
and lost their lives. It is reported that when the artist
Davyd Chychkan went to war, he said, "I am no better
than those others who are fighting on the front line,"
which literally meant, "They are the ones who have
it the hardest right now, and I will join them."

When the body of the artist and anarchist Davyd Chychkan lay in an open coffin on Independence Square, the site of the Ukrainian revolutions, there were many people and flags around: anarchist, feminist, LGBTQ, and Ukrainian. Printed copies of Davyd's works—his drawings—were in a row next to the coffin. Later, these pictures were moved to the cemetery, where the last farewell and burial took place with numerous people, friends, and relatives. Shortly before Davyd went to fight, his new exhibition was canceled by the Odesa National Art Museum due to threats from the artist's far-right opponents: his works featured anarchists and so-called "non-authoritarian leftists," fellows who are fighting for Ukraine or were killed in action. It was a project about the diversity of political views in the Ukrainian army, about the fact that the defenders of Ukraine feel responsible for how they would like to see their country.

In one of his works, Davyd depicted the image of Ukraine, for which he sacrificed his life: "Independent, autonomous, anti-authoritarian, classless, progressive, feminist, social, socialist." This vision of the future, described by Davyd in his radically utopian manner, will forever be intertwined with the memory of him. The future that will be rebuilt by those who remain, those who knew Davyd, will be illuminated by it. This forward-looking thought is, in fact, inspired by the past: the drawing that accompanies this inscription depicts prominent Ukrainian thinkers of the past—Mykhailo Drahomanov, Lesia Ukrainka, and Ivan Franko.[2]

The Independence Square gathered the entire artistic community present in Kyiv that day, and more. Hanna Tsyba, Davyd's wife and my friend, stood near the coffin, and their eight-month-old son Nestor slept nearby in a baby cart. I saw adult men sobbing. I, on the other hand, felt numbness; everything around me, the whole cityscape, was flooded with pain, yet I somehow couldn't feel that pain myself. It was lost in a way some people lost their sense of taste during COVID. I even found myself asking, where is it, the pain? In the days after I learned that Davyd was killed, I sometimes broke out crying; the wound seemed to open occasionally, the pain came in fits, and it happened often. I think it is obvious to many: Davyd remains with us in our memory, as well as in his drawings. Since the death of an artist, we always look at their work a little differently. Surprisingly, their works relieve the pain of loss; they are like a crust of dried blood protecting the wound inflicted by their death.

Inside, we are filled with blood; that means we are filled with life. Loss of blood, a bleeding wound, is a sign that death has come close. In the artwork painted with blood by artist Marharyta Polovinko, death lingers beside the man with an almost everyday closeness. Marharyta, who decided to fight at the front, left two mediums for her drawings: a simple pencil, which she used to draw angels screaming in response to every child killed by the Russians, and her blood. After the death of Marharyta in the summer of 2025, her drawings made in blood have changed color: in the ones published online during her lifetime, the color of blood is brighter. In the photos of the originals taken after her death, their color is a dark brown: blood, once separated from the body, changes its tone over time; it exists on its own.

Blood as an artistic medium leads us to confront a formula that has become ordinary and routine in wartime: you are either still alive or already dead. This formula takes the complexity and diversity of life experience out of focus, simplifying it to one constant: "You're still alive." Nothing else matters from what is left on the side of life. In this way, death seizes the territory of life while life is still ongoing. It seems to take away the sense of taste, the sense of pain. Likewise, at night during shelling, my fear disperses—it's somewhere around me, everywhere, yet I can no longer grasp whether I'm actually scared or not—I feel only the tension running through my whole body. After a night of shelling, scrolling through the news about destruction and deaths in the city, I feel neither shocked nor surprised—just the same numbness I felt at Davyd's funeral.

Yet, there is no greater comfort after a sleepless night of bombardment than stepping out into the streets of Kyiv and seeing people with purpose in their stride, others walking their dogs, and still others sipping coffee on benches or in cafés. Outside, there is life—and the fear begins to fade from the apartment the moment you open the curtains and the windows. Small ordinary actions and things come back to life, even though Russian missiles flew at us through the night carrying death with them. Small ordinary actions and things also cover the wound of an anxious night with that healing crust of dried blood.

Art now often addresses everyday things. Kyiv curator and psychologist Dana Brezhnieva and photographer Natalka Diachenko are jointly carrying out a long-term art project, "Dana and Natalka's Atelier of Wonders." It extends beyond the boundaries of art into everyday women's lives. They started the project in 2023 in the Zakarpattia region, working with displaced persons. Visiting the Atelier of Wonders, women get facial treatments and makeup, followed by a photo session. During this process, conversations unfold about life, experiences of war and stress, and the possibility of caring for oneself amid all of this.

In the spring of 2025, the Atelier traveled to the front line territories in the East of Ukraine and worked in cities in the Donetsk region: Kramatorsk, Sloviansk, and Sviatohirsk. Women and teenage girls, residents of partially destroyed front-line cities, received care sessions. Their photo portraits later became part of their home archive and part of the artists' portfolio. Artists write in their report about the trip, "It's not about appearance, it's about how we can regain ourselves through physicality, image, and touch of beauty." Giving moments of joy to others, Dana and Natalka get them in return: "For us, the Atelier is also a kind of rehabilitation and a way to focus on valuable mundane moments."[3]

In February 2025, I came to visit curator Oleksandra Pogrebniak for an apartment exhibition in her private home, on the left bank of the Dnipro river in Kyiv. Apartment exhibitions have become increasingly common in recent times; sometimes as one-off events in someone's home and sometimes as ongoing projects, such as those held in artist Tamara Turliun's apartment, or in the Balcony Gallery in the Podil district, organized by curator Oksana Ozarchuk.

Sasha Pogrebniak has a two-year-old son, Teo, and her husband recently got mobilized into the army.[4] It so happened that her birthday falls on February 24—the day Russia launched its full-scale war against us. Sasha decided that instead of celebrating her birthday each year (how can one "celebrate" when it now marks the start of the full-scale war?), she would hold an annual home exhibition on this date, dedicated to the war's

anniversary, and open her doors to guests for this public event.

Art becomes a protective crust over the wound inflicted on the most intimate holiday.

I was brought to one such exhibition by artist and curator Maryna Marynichenko. Entering the apartment, we saw artworks displayed on the walls of a large living room, and a group of people gathered at the entrance to the bathroom. I peek over the shoulders and heads and see, from behind, the artist Katia Libkind sitting at a small table in the bathroom, scrolling through her laptop and sorting through her personal digital archive (a "digital compost," as she later described it in a private conversation). Katia Libkind, together with another artist, Katia Buchatska, has been working with neurodivergent individuals for several years. They plan to open an art space dedicated to their creative practices.

I notice a stain of blood on the bathroom floor. Since everyone is standing in silence and no one is explaining anything, I only learn later from one of the guests what is actually happening. Stepping further into the bathroom, I finally see the scene myself: as Katia scrolls through the folders on her laptop, a catheter is attached to her arm. It is connected by a tube with a transparent medical bag filled with blood hanging on the wall. As was explained to me, the blood was taken from one hand, and then redirected back into the body through the other hand. The action resembles a medical procedure, an act of self-destruction, or self-sacrifice. At first, I can't understand why the artist is doing this to her own body for the sake of art—since in the event announcement it is described as a performance. The performance is titled *Angel Folding the Sky.*[5]

     On Blood and the Most Radical Gesture of Care

Blood sampling into the bag and returning it to the body (the amount of blood sampled reached 450 ml) lasted about thirty minutes. Afterward, the audience and the artist left the bathroom and settled in a large hall. Sasha, the curator, greeted the guests with a welcoming word. I sat on the floor next to Katia asking what this performance meant to her. Although I have had my own interpretations, mixed with feelings of sublimity, fear, and disgust, I am always curious to hear what an artist has to say about their work.

Katia replied briefly and simply that the work carried no special meaning, beyond the literal idea of stepping out of her own body and then returning into it. In fact, this act is an exercise Katia learned during the Hospitallers' combat medic training.[6] I learned that a blood transfusion, which may need to be performed on another person, is something the medics practice on themselves. This simple, matter-of-fact explanation lowered the level of fear in my initial perception of the work and revealed it instead as a practice of care and a crucial skill adapted for wartime.

Under the pressure of war, the artist has effectively acquired the qualifications of a field medic—stepping far beyond the boundaries of artistic practice. Katia shared that while mastering this exercise, she saw the transfusion as a pure, self-contained, and fully realized artistic gesture. The performance itself presents that gesture—in the artist's words, "this work is a pure form."

The apartment exhibition marking the anniversary of the war's beginning and the blood-transfusion performance are both artistic responses to the war. Here, art practices are both a departure from the body and a return to it—as well as the reclaiming of one's own birthday within the warmth of a community expending the significance of the date. Sasha Pogrebniak comments on her exhibition project:

> *In this new reality, I see these apartment exhibitions as a feminist form of reclaiming private space—not as a withdrawal, but as a site where care, reflection, and artistic thought can coexist, offering an individualized form of resistance, and a way to stay present amidst ongoing rupture.*[7]

Among the other books on the bookshelf in Sasha Pogrebniak's apartment, I find the catalogue of the *Ukrainian Body* exhibition that I curated in 2012, together with Lesia Kulchynska. The exhibition, which was located at the Visual Culture Research Center, then at the Kyiv Mohyla Academy, was shut down by the university's president, Serhii Kvit, because of several works dealing with sexuality and body.

I take the catalogue from the shelf to show those present work by Oleksandr Volodarskyi, *Green Bottle Filled with Red Liquid* (2012), we had included in the exhibition. It was a bottle filled with his own blood, placed on a shelf, accompanied by video documentation of how he took his own blood. The work was dedicated to political prisoners. Oleksandr became such a prisoner in 2011, after he was arrested near the Verkhovna Rada during a nude performance: he and a friend simulated sexual intercourse near a state institution. The performance was a protest against the actions of the National Expert Commission for the Protection of Morals during the presidency of Viktor Yanukovych, which censored films and books on the topics of corporeality, sexuality, and LGBTQ experiences. A few days after the Ukrainian Body exhibition was shut down, Lesia Kulchynska and I went back into the space and found the bottle lying on the floor beside a dark, brownish stain of blood on the wooden boards. We never learned how it happened, but we were struck by the symbolic coincidence—blood had been spilled at the exhibition both literally and metaphorically, as if in response to an act of restricting freedom of expression.

As we flipped through the catalogue, sitting on the floor at Sasha's apartment, a bridge formed between one artwork about blood and another, created thirteen years apart. These works belong to different moments in time, yet to a single Ukrainian art history—a history of many forms of resistance and of the struggle for our freedom. The war cuts the past away; at times it is difficult to connect yesterday with today, let alone link the previous decade to the present. Yet recently, art researchers Milena Khomchenko and Tania Zhmurko asked me to write a text about my curatorial projects from the period between the two revolutions— the decade 2004–14. They are working on a book dedicated to the art of that era. I am writing that text for them and, simultaneously, writing this one. This is, in fact, another thing we do in Ukraine during the war: we document our turbulent art history for future generations.

I do not want to allow the war to cast its shadow over me and freeze my memory, to reshape my perception in a way that makes me self-censor or hide things that may seem "unimportant" today. This is difficult, because our relationship with death—which is now so close—is double-edged: what it wants (and behind it stands the Russian aggressor) is to strip both small and significant things of their meaning. Its formula is simple: you are either still alive or already dead—a maximally reduced version of life that pushes the entire complexity and richness of human experience out of view. But what we set against it—and this is another aspect of our relationship with death (the mastery of not giving up)—is the act of assigning meaning to significant things and to small things, to everyday gestures and to fantasies, to the history of the country and to history of its art.

Life reveals itself when something gains meaning. Everything that life is filled with can give us the strength to keep living. Life is in the new makeup that Dana and Natalka gifted to the women of a city shattered by Russian shelling. Life is inviting friends into one's home—to an exhibition that is also a birthday gathering. Life is in caring for a child, as Hanna cares for Nestor, whose father was killed in the war. Her daily caring routine will always exist in the light of the most radical gesture made by Davyd, Maryna, and other artists who joined so many defenders—many of them far removed from the art world—on the front line. Many of them will never come back. Through their care, they saved the lives of others.

Everything that life is filled with can give us the strength to keep living. There is a certain power of self-renewal in all this—like blood that leaves the body and then returns to it. To step outside oneself and then come back is a formula suggested by the training of blood transfusion, a skill meant to save a life. The most important return we all long for is the return to peaceful life, when the tyrant, the aggressor, the enemy is finally defeated.

     On Blood and the Most Radical Gesture of Care

Blood can clot, forming a protective layer over a wound—one of the body's basic survival mechanisms. Gestures that step beyond the boundaries of art eventually return something to art itself: the capacity to become a protective skin that covers a wound. Today, in Ukraine, art serves precisely as such a protective crust for the mental wounds inflicted by the war.

October, 2025 ●

Oksana Briukhovetska is an artist, curator, researcher and writer from Kyiv, Ukraine. She is an editor of Ukrainian women artists' projects collection *Meaning after Loss* (2025) and an author of the book *Black Lives Matter Voices* (Choven, 2025).

1   *Art Stitches Ruptured Time Back Together: Introduction in the Meaning After Loss*, edited by Oksana Briukhovetska. Martin Roth Initiative, 2025. Online access: https: //www.martin-roth-initiative.de/en/ukrainian-women-artists-publication.

2   Mykhailo Drahomanov, Lesya Ukrainka, and Ivan Franko are canonical figures in Ukrainian literature and philosophical thought of the late nineteenth and early twentieth centuries, associated with national-democratic and socialist views.

3   "The probability that I will die is 0.01%": the adventures of the Photoatelier of Wonders in the Donetsk region. https://artslooker.com/virohidnist-toho-shcho-ia-zahynu-0-01-pryhody-fotoatelie-chudes-na-donechchyni/.

4   Sasha Pogrebnyak's husband, Dmytro Chepurnyi, is also a curator in civilian life.

5   The performance was multi-layered—at the same time, pieces of canvas with the artist's painted sky studies were tumbling in the washing machine nearby, while in the bathroom sink, amid soap foam, floated the bodily remnants of another performance shown in the exhibition on video: glitter, pubic hair, and white false eyelashes.

6   The Hospitallers are a Ukrainian volunteer medical battalion that has been taking part in the Russian–Ukrainian war in the Donbas since 2014. It provides first medical and pre-medical aid, as well as evacuation of wounded Ukrainian soldiers from the hottest sections of the frontline. (https://uk.wikipedia.org/wiki/).

7   Oleksandra Pogrebnyak. *On Peace and Joy from an Apartment Exhibition in Kyiv*. https://mostmagazine.org/2025/10/13/on-peace-and-joy-from-an-apartment-exhibition-in-kyiv/.

          On Blood and the Most Radical Gesture of Care

Denny's Garages

Arina Yanovych

Between Ruins and Resilience

There is a truth both cruel and consoling: life continues—even through war. Beneath the wail of sirens and the endless scroll of news and numbers, the human need for meaning, for beauty, for a fleeting sense of normalcy, persists. Life itself breaks through the smoke, refusing to be extinguished.

Even ruins speak of this persistence. They are not only remains, but beginnings—thresholds of what has yet to take form. Every collapse contains the outline of renewal. To rebuild a city is not merely to repair its walls; it is to decide what a society chooses to remember, and what it is willing to lose.

But how can urban development for the benefit of all take root in a society when survival itself is the only plan?

Since the late 1980s, cities around the world have been shaped by the same equation: more land, more profit. In Ukraine—and most visibly in Kyiv—this logic became gospel throughout the 1990s and continues to define construction, even amid war. Yet the edges of this system are fraying. There are places urban planning forgot: sites that resist commodification, where a different kind of city life quietly endures. In contrast to polished façades and speculative towers, these in-between zones hold onto something human. They are not ruins of the past but living counterproposals: fragments of another possible city, one that values connection over capital.

20 m² of Freedom

It began, as many Soviet stories had, with a shortage. In the 1950s, the private car became a symbol of progress—a personal victory within the collective project. The state encouraged ownership as a marker of modernity and stability, but failed to provide any parking spaces.

From this gap, garage cooperatives emerged: self-organized associations that built and managed their own storage spaces on the city's margins. Joining these cooperatives was slow—entangled in paperwork, waiting lists, and favors. Officially, each garage was merely a box for a car. Unofficially, it was a doorway.

Behind steel doors, life unfolded in parallel: workshops, hideouts, clubs, spaces for solitude and small gatherings. What began as pure utility evolved into a network of private worlds—each filled with tools, furniture, photos, collections, and small histories. Amid the monotony of Soviet housing, these structures became places of difference. They offered a modest but radical freedom: to make, to tinker, to exist outside the plan. In their everyday practices, they carried a quiet resistance—the insistence that life could still be one's own.

Garage Nation

The Kyianivskyi Garage Cooperative sits high on one of Kyiv's hills, between Vozdvyzhenka and Peizazhna Alley—an improbable enclave where gentrification, ruin, and wilderness overlap. The path to it winds between manicured façades and overgrown plots, past half-collapsed villas and trees reclaiming the slope. At the top lies a plateau with the first rows of garages. Some are two stories high, clinging to the hillside. Their brutalist frames remain, softened by moss and vines. Soviet concrete mingles with decades of improvisation.

Denny was among the first to recognize potential here rather than decay. With no budget and no formal plan, he simply began. In early 2025, together with friends, he started renting and clearing individual garages, gradually repurposing them as open studios,

Denny's Garages

event spaces, refuges, and repair cafés. Inside, material traces of earlier lives remain: photo paper from the 1990s, rolls of film, broken tools, and tiles worn smooth by years of use.

Once again, the garages have become spaces of encounter—unfixed, self-organizing, alive. There are music sessions, small exhibitions, tea gatherings, repair cafés, and late-night conversations that stretch into dawn. What emerges is not a project but a rhythm of shared presence: neighbors, artists, and students, each bringing something to the mix. Among the younger generation, especially, there is a hunger for places like this—spaces where togetherness can be practiced, not prescribed. In these temporary spaces of solidarity, a new urban ethic begins to take shape.

Denny once showed an old floor plan of the complex: a grid of rectangular buildings, axially aligned, with no discernible hierarchy. The plan appears sober and technical. Each garage is numbered, some additionally marked with street names—including Kyianivskyi Provulok, which still exists today. In the center is a slightly larger building, marked on the map as the "Security Building." The idea of a small urban village with a communal center is still palpable today.

Such encounters between wilderness and architecture are vanishing from contemporary cities. Kyianivskyi remains a rare palimpsest: Soviet foundations, archaeological fragments, and yesterday's graffiti. Seemingly accidental, yet precise in its layering, it serves as a living archive of urban memory.

But this fragile ecology stands at risk. The city's vision of "modernization" promises order: smooth asphalt, flowerbeds, and floodlights. Clean, safe, and empty. Against this, Denny's community proposes

something quieter but deeper: to preserve the site as
a public urban garden, a place where nature and culture
cohabit. The aim is to create planted areas and spaces
for community activities—with tree species that attract
urban birds and promote local biodiversity.

Denny's practice creates an aesthetic of necessity
and recalls the original idea of garage cooperatives:
communal action within limited resources. "Kyianivskyi"
is an example of a whole series of similar projects
that respond to the lack of public infrastructure—and
to mistrust of often corrupt state planning.

(Sur)real Estate

From the plateau of the garage cooperative, there is
a view of the newly built residential quarters. The new
Vozdvizhenka district is considered one of the most
striking examples of failed urban development: an
eclectic mix of architectural styles and references—
without any recognizable concept. Pastel-colored,
ornamented façades, different roof shapes, French
balconies, and postmodern elements are jarring due
to their lack of scale and connection to their surround-
ings. What is referred to here as the "old town" is
a constructed simulation—architecture as pure surface,
detached from historical consciousness and social
life. Against this simulation, the garages stand out
as stubbornly real.

While investment projects chase profit and specta-
cle, the garage cooperative follows another economy—
an aesthetic of necessity. Here, culture grows from
what is at hand: reclaimed, improvised, and shared.[1]
It resists the world Baudrillard warned of—the city
as simulacrum[2]—by remaining grounded in use, in care,
and in the friction of the everyday.

These spaces are porous and adaptable; they allow the real to exist. Culture here is not curated but lived—arising from proximity, conflict, and play. A new urban sensibility begins where the plan ends and life takes over.

How long such places can exist before they are absorbed by commercial profit-making logic is uncertain. However, their power lies precisely in their transience: they are fluid, resistant, open—spaces that show that cultural development is not linear but cyclical. When they disappear, more is lost than their physical presence. With them disappears the possibility of living culture beyond prefabricated norms—places where sharing is not staged but practiced.

Perhaps Denny—real or symbolic—is less a figure than a principle: the insistence on autonomy, on action and presence. With him returns the essential question: Who owns the city, and which of its possible futures are still worth fighting for today? ●

1   Similar urban processes have unfolded elsewhere. In 1980s Detroit, abandoned buildings became sanctuaries for cultural communities seeking safe space—eventually forming a movement with global influence. In post-reunification Berlin, unused lots gave rise to a diverse club and cultural scene that shaped the city's image and, in current day, generates over €1.5 billion annually, according to studies.

2   The term simulacrum comes from Jean Baudrillard's *Simulacra and Simulation* (1981), where he argues that in postmodern society, representations become detached from the real. In place of authenticity emerges a simulation—a copy without an original, a reality replaced by illusion.

Arina Yanovych is an architect and researcher based in Berlin. Her work focuses on the preservation, activation, and transformation of (industrial) areas.

Olives

In this lucid March darkness, in this airy prelude to April,
when everyone blossoms as best they can, in the brown
    box of the train carriage,
as smooth as a bud scale, yes, yes, little girl
painted olives of the world in her book,
because someone once said that after misfortune,
    a dove would bring
an olive branch, but I think, Mama, that she should rather
have brought a whole jar of olives, for salad. Yes, yes.

As in ancient myths, our rough, abandoned villages of
    the north appeared,
with bushy brows of dead wood, the fields passed by.
    Still far to the
south. Yes, yes.
Towards the south, only birds formed their flocks freely.
    Spring stood victorious in
the air.
Ours. Native. In a fabulously green historical manuscript
    on the black
pages of the conflagration. The dove circled around
    without finding the wild olive and instead carried
a silvery marble into your dream. Yes, yes.

Julia Stakhivska, 2023

The Occupation Reflex

Oleksii Minko

I must avoid metaphors when talking about the occupation. Otherwise, there is a risk of losing the right to talk about it. To betray the occupation, to surrender to the challenge it poses. This is what I learned from academic discourse and the ethics of research. "Decolonization is not a metaphor,"[1] so I shouldn't use any.

I must remember how the occupiers create infrastructure based on combining "their" and "my" technologies, looking at the factuality of its dynamics. I must distinguish between them, and build my argument by following Russian remnants on the battlefield and in the occupied territories. I must see the potential in practices, and not allow the threat to capture it and be subjugated to the Russian version of the future. I should stay balanced and focused on evidence, abstaining from exaggeration. I must be a cold interface in the hot phase of war. I must imagine only what I have heard from loved ones or investigative journalists. The occupation shapes my ethics through the negative, through what is inaccessible to me, through what I know less about, what I have no option to know better and no right to spread further, endangering people there.[2]

I must remain silent about what I do not know. When I do not restrain myself, I am a traitor. In the eyes of a traitor, the occupation spreads on both sides of the line of combat. The defense forces are unable to restrain it. The spaces that the Russians have entered are now different. In them, atoms live in convulsions.

In the Ukrainian case, eschatology[3] is an empirical science. The end of the world is a bunch of everyday statistics, calculations of resources and experiments of pushing the limits of the condition, successful or failed. I will find a way to remain cold. After all, what I must remain silent about in the language of science, the language of fact, convincing research, judgment, and proof. I can try not to use language, but rather use the whimpering of a victim, who in his agony, repeats the words of his executioner. I will parody what the killer wants to hear. On his terms, according to his ambitions. Let him win. The killer wants to win so badly. He will say everything through my mouth, and he will speak metaphorically.

> *Pavlov's disobedient dog.[4] This dog will behave as required. We will prepare her for our arrival. Turn off the lights.*

Russians move around in an armored personnel carrier near a shopping center. There is a line in front of it. There is no light inside. People are waiting for "humanitarian aid" stored in the premises. There are buses around with screens on their roofs, depicting how to get new documents, and with them new SIM cards.

Many faces, unfamiliar to locals, appear.

Damaged buildings are being demolished, and similar new ones are appearing—with brightly colored balconies. Along with them—monuments to fallen soldiers. Somewhere between them, the dictator drives around in his car.

Local museums are beginning to review their exhibits and reorganize. Only what cannot be moved will remain—the buildings themselves, the churches. Little will change in the museum dedicated to the events of World War II. What has been crossed out with a marker will be redrawn.

Children often go to summer camps where they learn tactics, first aid, and the basics of drone control. They are trained to compete against each other. A specially built training ground will host the games. With weapons, military equipment, simulated shell explosions, tanks, video broadcasts, and points awarded for successfully completing game tasks. Actually, it's not really a summer camp, but a military training polygon for children. At the end of their (often forceful) visit, the children are asked to share their impressions on camera. They say they feel rested, and ready to return to the camp again. Their next trip will take place as part of their military service.

At first, Russian pop stars will perform on open-air stages. Ruins are visible in the background. The main audience is the camera, or rather those who watch the news report. Later, there will only be symphony concerts, Accordion Day, and Victory Days in the Spring, Summer, Fall, and Winter. Photos from these events will remain on deserted Telegram channels.

I have to wait for information from friends about traveling abroad. When I try, I am not allowed to leave. And then the familiar restrictions begin: mobilization. Voluntary or compulsory—it doesn't matter. Restrictions on movement. "A state in a smartphone."[5] Social agreement. Social consent. No elections. Wash when there is electricity. Read when there is no electricity.

The dog sits in the dark.

Reports of filtration camps, deportation, re-education of children, eviction of Ukrainians from their homes, torture, murder. Surveillance and persecution, military registration. News about Russian successes on the front lines. Waiting for partners and spouses of active military personnel. Russian shelling, deaths. This is the advancing of the occupation.

Information travels. Pieces of construction debris fill the room after an explosion. The story of debris hitting the house passes from ear to ear, and so on.[6] Dust particles of information comprise terror and control. The Russians summon the demon of bits and pieces, both in spiritual and material dimensions, sweeping away all living things on the earth's surface. A single movement of its paw adds them to its own realm.

If occupation occurs somewhere, it occurs everywhere. The relationship between 'here' and 'there' becomes tense when it arrives and does not relax. They amortize. The bodies attached to these relationships swell.[7]

This is a society of telepaths. Its members share common knowledge which they sing into each other's minds to feel unity. This gives them headaches, and during the intervals between songs, people begin to whisper. They doubt some of the lyrics and argue about their interpretation and whether they are in tune. The demon is persistent, and when the telepaths' voices break and only murmurs remain, his whispering will be the loudest.

The more buffer zones the demon creates between what has been taken away and what is being defended, the greater the temptation to let go. In an imperialist casino, the colonized have to gamble everything away. For internally displaced persons, war is a telekinetic experience. They hold physical objects many kilometers away, as a form of resistance.

No more, no less: keeping your virtual avatar in enemy territory at night while breaking through the demonic telefrontier each time.

Turn on the light. Is your saliva dripping?

A dream. I find myself in Moscow for a couple of days. I walk the same streets, somewhere not quite in the

   The Occupation Reflex

center of the city. Some buildings are damaged by Ukrainian drones. I worry that passersby will peek at my phone when a message in Ukrainian appears on it. People on the bus already noticed my accent. Walking through the park (Why am I walking around? What am I supposed to find here?), a Russian man is handed a military draft notice on a parallel street. The same thing could happen to me at any moment. When does my bus leave from here? Won't they check my documents when I leave?

Another dream. There is little light in Zaporizhia. For some reason, KFC is open (was there ever a KFC in Zaporizhia, and if so, how can it be open?). The air raid siren starts wailing. How can I protect myself from a KAB bomb attack? There is an underpass nearby, so I need to stay close to it in case the city is targeted. I'm hungry. When will the alarm on my phone ring?

In terms of frequency, dreams about my hometown are outnumbered by dreams about Moscow. Perhaps dreams about the occupation start when I wake up to the sound of shelling. From time to time, I daydream about it in the form of writing, conversation or performance. At such moments, I don't dream about the occupation: I speak about distances, time differences, mirages and anxious premonitions—generally, about relationships despite obstacles.

I once noticed that my grandmother's time under occupation was not 7 p.m. like mine, for example, but 8 p.m. Sometimes it was the other way around, with it being 12 p.m. for me and 11 p.m. for her. One year, Ukrainian time is ahead and Russian time is behind; the next year, it's the other way around. The difference could be not just one hour, but several. When an armed meridian cut off our communication, did my grandmother and I have more or less time together?

The fear of not being able to escape Russian danger in dreams is similar in intensity to the desire to eat my grandmother's khachapuri.[8] When will the alarm ring?

The straps are squeezing the dog's body. The dog moves around more.

I dreamed of attacks on Ukrainian cities and advances in a village in the Sumy region—but I did not dream of occupied Kyiv, Kharkiv, or Dnipro. The occupation of Ukraine as a whole may not be so spectacular. For some, life will be reduced to hiding and trying to avoid certain bureaucratic procedures. For others, it will lead to a visit to the courthouse, subsequently a prison cell, or a quick death following the violent dispersal of a protest.

Will I dare to throw a Molotov cocktail at an armored personnel carrier on the street of a regional center if I have not yet dared to engage in combat with ammunition, firearm in my hand, artillery and air support? Will I dare to avoid exchanging my Ukrainian passport for a Russian one if I plan to evade service in the Ukrainian army after my deferment ends this summer? Will I dare to stay if I can leave? Will I be able to kill myself if I am forcibly drafted into the Russian Armed Forces? Is it possible to be so resilient as to avoid collaboration? Is it possible to be so irresponsible as to agree to it?

The dog is untied from its straps. It lies down at its owner's feet.

Bulgakov was wrong about the ending of *Heart of a Dog*.[9] In the story, a professor named Preobrazhensky turns a dog into a human, but after a lot of trouble, he turns the human back into a dog. Here's how I see it:

The Occupation Reflex

the dog that the professor had humanized found a way
to turn the professor himself into a dog. He learned
how to perform a special operation and did so. Even at
gunpoint, the dog-professor did not lie on its back in
a sign of submission. This was partly due to its nobility
and partly due to the annoying fleas on its skin.

Do dogs really feel guilty when they are scolded for
disobeying commands? And when they are praised, are
they really happy about it? A Ukrainian dog who is only
concerned with how special she is and where her food
comes from reveals her insincere loyalty.[10]

The subject of occupation is distasteful to everyone,
including itself. Russians are uncertain about its loyalty,
which is why so much effort is expended to persuade it.
The subject can also cause doubt among the Ukrainian
defenders: what if the subject has been turned into
a traitor? The subject of occupation is tormented by the
choice to stay occupied. The subject is tormented by
the expectation that it may slip up when demonstrating
loyalty to Russians, or go too far in playing the role
of a collaborator, betraying the Ukrainian people. Its
ambivalence threatens all fighting sides. For the subject, the space between doubt and choice subverts any
order that emerges from the compression of war.

*A whistle sounds. The dog is electrocuted.
It is paralyzed. Whining can be heard. The electric
shocks become stronger.*

Do dogs dream about the future? ●

Oleksii Minko is an artist, researcher, member of the research collective
Occupational Formations: Infrastructures of the Seen and Unseen.

1   "Decolonization is not a metaphor"—is a name of the academic paper
    by Eve Tuck and K. Wayne Yang, in which they criticize the superficial
    understanding of decolonization and advocates for decolonization as
    a specific action: return of the occupied land to the Indigenous people.
    Tuck, Eve; Yang, K. Wayne (2012). "Decolonization is not a metaphor."
    Decolonization: Indigeneity, Education & Society. 1 (1): 1–40.

2   These thoughts came from the conversations we had with Vlada
    Vazheyevsky within the working group "Occupational Formations:
    Infrastructures of Seen and Unseen."

3   Eschatology is a theological doctrine in monotheistic traditions that
    articulates beliefs about the ultimate destiny of the world and humanity,
    including the end of times, the Apocalypse, and the Last Judgment.

4   Ivan Pavlov (September 14, 1849—February 27, 1936) was a Russian
    physiologist known for his work on the concept of conditioned reflexes.
    He conducted experiments on the nervous system of dogs. In his
    most famous experiment, a hungry dog was trained to salivate in
    response to the sound of a buzzer, which was systematically
    sounded before feeding.

5   This is the slogan associated with Diia, a Ukrainian app that makes
    governmental services accessible to citizens via their smartphones.
    Since the Ukrainian Ministry of Defence developed an app for con-
    trolling military conscription, the phrase previously associated with
    positive changes is now used in an ironic way.

6   These observations are inspired by the text of Svitlana Matviyenko.
    "Terror Environment." https://theater.spatialtech.info/en/essays/
    terror-environment.

7   Inspired by Asia Bazdyrieva lecture within the educational program
    titled "Daily Inner Genius of War" conducted by Valeria Malchenko in
    collaboration with Work In Progress (w.i.p) community.

8   Khachapuri is a Georgian dish that has several variations. Generally,
    it is a cheese-filled bread. Often filled with suluguni, elastic Georgian
    brined cheese.

9   *Heart of a Dog* is a novel by Kyiv-born writer Mikhail Bulgakov.
    Written in 1925, it satirically depicts early Soviet society. The novel
    tells the story of a stray dog that is transformed into a human
    by a famous surgeon professor but is later turned back into a dog
    after behaving unethically.

10 In Franz Kafka's novel *The Investigation of a Dog*, the narrative is told
    from the perspective of a dog-researcher who, among other things,
    seeks answers to the question "Whence does the Earth procure its food?".

                                    The Occupation Reflex

A Record of War Fatigue

Yelizaveta Landenberger

February 24, 2022 – Morning

I wake up from a restless sleep around five in the morning, in my (former) apartment in Czechia, and immediately look at my cellphone. For weeks, I have been glued to the screen, constantly reading news, Telegram channels, Twitter threads. My worst fears have come true: the war has begun.

I desperately write to friends in Ukraine offering to help them in any way—as well as to friends in Russia, asking them to do something.

According to Hannah Arendt, the two terms "power" and "violence" are mistakenly conflated, with violence being seen as "the most flagrant manifestation of power."[1]

Arendt disagrees. Violence is used where power crumbles. The terms are, in fact, opposites. "Where the one rules absolutely, the other is absent."[2]

February 24, 2022 – Evening

A large demonstration march in Prague. Protesters—Ukrainians, Belarusians, Russians, Georgians, but mostly Czechs—throw eggs at the display window in front of the Russian embassy, chanting slogans such as "Putin fuck you," while police officers stand by smiling. Someone has wrapped toilet paper with Putin's face printed on it around the embassy fence. A banner reads in Czech, impressing me with its clarity: *"Invaze je zlo"*—"The invasion is evil." There is a sense of togetherness in the air, an intoxicating feeling of solidarity that permeates and mobilizes body and mind. The memory of 1968 seems alive—the Prague Spring. The blossoming of democracy, and its subsequent suppression by Warsaw Pact troops. The images of Soviet tanks in Prague have not faded from people's minds even after more than half a century.

"Violence [...] is distinguished by its instrumental character. Phenomenologically, it is close to strength, since the implements of violence, like all other tools, are designed and used for the purpose of multiplying natural strength until, in the last stage of their development, they can substitute for it."[3]

According to Arendt, the suppression of the Prague Spring was a "text book case of a confrontation between violence and power in their pure states."[4]

Russia's large-scale invasion of Ukraine is another one, and Putin has clearly not read Arendt. He was unable to establish a power base through disinformation, attacks, and support for separatists in Eastern and Southern Ukraine. On the contrary, Russia became increasingly unpopular there because of the war in Donbas, which tore apart families and destroyed numerous lives. Since Putin had no power, he resorted to violence—in the mistaken belief that this is the pinnacle of power.

February 25, 2022

Upon arriving in Berlin, I am overwhelmed by the absence of war. The people on the streets and in the cafés seem carefree, everything appears normal. The large influx of refugees has not yet arrived.

In the days that follow, I sort donations for the refugees. They will be able to stock up on essentials—snacks, soap, toothbrushes—at a kind of free store. Other donations are brought to Western Ukraine by trucks. Some of the items that Berliners have donated are unusable. Some of the fabrics are unwashed and full of holes. I come across a used comb with tufts of hair still stuck between the bristles—almost as if someone had disposed of their rubbish here.

February 27, 2022

A large demonstration for peace in Ukraine in the center
of Berlin. According to the police, there were 100,000
participants, but it felt more like half a million. I am glad
that German society is not indifferent to the war after all.

Then I see posters emblazoned with doves, peace
signs, and slogans against weapons, and I realize that
two different factions with opposing goals have gathered on this day. One condemns the Russian invasion
and demands consistent sanctions against the aggressor. The others—supposed pacifists—believe that the
Ukrainians should surrender.

They do not understand what occupation means.
Unlike the Czechs, part of the German population
never experienced the violence of Soviet rule. The other
part—those from the East—seem at times to indulge
in nostalgic feelings, having forgotten the realities
of totalitarianism.

November 30, 2022

Where the Russian troops later retreat, it becomes
clear what atrocities they are capable of: the streets
of Bucha, the forests of Izium, the torture chambers
of Kherson.

October 17, 2022

At the Literaturhaus Berlin, Jakob Augstein, owner
and publisher of the left-wing weekly newspaper
Der Freitag, talks to Vienna-based Ukrainian writer
Tanya Malyarchuk. I listen to the conversation on
the radio. Augstein's arrogance gives me second-hand
embarrassment:

I always had the feeling that I was growing up in a wounded, injured city. […] My dead father had a strange scar on his arm. There was an entry wound here and an exit wound there […] The war was present in our lives, in my life. You're probably thinking that you're dealing with some kind of spoiled, soft Western asshole. But what you don't know is what the war means to me in my biography and in my background, so to speak. […] That means I'm really, truly afraid of war, really afraid.

Augstein uses this position as a spokesperson to emphasize how important it is to avoid an escalation of the war. But his comments on Paris are the most gruesome: how fortunate that it was not defended militarily during World War II, because otherwise this city would no longer exist. He believes that Kyiv should not defend itself either, and instead be conquered.

He seems unaware that it was the Germans who reduced large parts of present-day Ukraine to rubble and ashes during World War II, which makes his analogy appear rather skewed. Augstein's core message is: I am tired of war and I am afraid. Stop it so I can have some peace and quiet.

Augstein is so self-absorbed that he pays no attention to how his conversation partner, who is directly affected by the war, must feel.

August 26, 2024

Sahra Wagenknecht, the then-leader of the BSW party[5] bearing her name, is touring ahead of the state elections in eastern Germany. Today she is speaking in her hometown of Jena. "And where we also need a major change, and this is really close to my heart,

A Record of War Fatigue

is the question of war and peace!" she shouts to the enthusiastic crowd.

I am there as a journalist. There are flyers printed in Russian, likely aimed at ethnic Germans—like me—who immigrated to Germany in the 1990s.

The solutions offered by populists are simple: lower rents, higher pensions. War off, peace on. No weapons to Ukraine, ergo peace.

At the end of the speech, there is a surprise: Ukrainian women stand in front of the stage with blue and yellow posters and chant: "Support Ukraine!" and "Stop the Russian war of aggression!" A reality shock for those present. They boo the war refugees and insult them: "Bums!," "Go home!," "Warmongers!" It is only thanks to the police officers that they do not become violent. The presence of war victims forces reality into the enchanted minds of Wagenknecht's supporters, threatening to destroy their worldview—and they push back against it.

On the same day, Ukraine suffers one of the most brutal Russian air strikes to date.

March 2, 2025

"I call it the Pokrovsk diet, 17 kilograms in 0.2 seconds," jokes Eddy Scott from his hospital bed. Eddy is a civilian, a volunteer. As part of the NGO Base UA, he evacuated people from areas close to the front line. I visit him as a journalist in a Kyiv hospital. He is tired, having lost his left leg and left arm a month ago, in a Russian FPV drone attack in the Donetsk region. Black humor helps him cope, he says.

What happened to Eddy is the everyday reality for civilians in Ukraine. Each such incident should shock us, yet it seems that fewer and fewer people truly take notice. According to a study from Germany, older voters and people with limited political interest are more prone to war fatigue and skepticism toward long-term military operations.[6]

August 10, 2025

As I wait for my pizza in Berlin, I read the news on Instagram: the artist Davyd Chychkan died on the front-line. I can't believe it. Just a week ago, he sent me a voice message, which I listen to again now. The new portrait I was supposed to write about him will never be written. Instead, I write an obituary through my tears.

October 2, 2025

I think of Mariupol, the port city that was destroyed by Russian troops in the first months of the war. Research by aid organizations shows that between March 2022 and February 2023, more than 10,000 people were buried, at least 8,000 of them as a result of fighting or war-related causes. The actual toll is probably far greater, with countless victims never recovered from the rubble. Russia is reconstructing the city over the very bones of those who once lived there, literally.

Talk shows, "peace demonstrations," and both left-wing and right-wing media outlets that refuse to show any solidarity with Ukrainians frequently use words such as "warmonger" or its synonym "bellicist." These terms are generally used to insult Ukrainians or people who show solidarity with the invaded country and demand clear consequences for Russia. Another word on this list is "war fatigue," in the way it is mostly used.

"We are tired of war!" reads a social media post by the left-wing party Die Linke in Saxony from early September. It states that peace is not achieved through

A Record of War Fatigue

more weapons, but through diplomacy, disarmament, and international cooperation. How is that supposed to work when the aggressor is not interested in peace at all?

Yet, a media induced war fatigue seems unavoidable, human: Day after day, we see images of burned-out houses and dead landscapes, soldiers with dirty faces and tired eyes. We read and hear the same stories of violence, suffering, and crime over and over again. Not only in Ukraine, but in other places around the world. Who still really takes in this information, who is still moved by it?

At the same time, Russia is running its war economy at full speed and air strikes on cities and civilian infrastructure are increasing. Even villages twenty kilometers from the front lines have become uninhabitable. The Russian army is sending more and more small quadcopter drones carrying explosives, hunting anything that moves.

We constantly hear that the people in Ukraine are war-weary. And yes, they have been exhausted for a long time. But what are they supposed to do?

To substitute violence for power can bring victory, but the price is very high, Arendt writes. "For it is not only paid by the vanquished, it is also paid by the victor in terms of his own power." She states, "Violence can destroy power, but it is completely incapable of creating it."[7] ●

Yelizaveta Landenberger is a research assistant at the Institute for Slavic Studies and Hungarian Studies at Humboldt University in Berlin and a freelance journalist.

1   Hannah Arendt, *On Violence* (New York: Harcourt, Brace & World, 1970), 38.

2   Ibid., 56.

3   Ibid., 46.

4   Ibid., 53.

5   A populist left-wing party founded in 2024.

6   https://www.dkjs.de/wp-content/uploads/2025/02/analyse-politische-einstellungen-und-wahlverhalten-junger-menschen.pdf.

7   Ibid., Arendt, 53.

War Time City Guide

Oleksandr Burlaka

The following text is a brief architectural guide to my hometown of Kyiv, informed by the events of Russia's attempted invasion in March 2022. Some topics are important and warrant more attention, while others can be mentioned briefly. Bear in mind that the situation continues to change while you are reading this guide.

Anxiety and Shelter

As I write this, the city administration has announced that it will begin installing mobile shelters. These basic concrete structures have become a familiar sight on the streets of Kharkiv, Sumy, and Dnipro—cities located closer to the Russian border or the front line. While these modular concrete shelters are useful as temporary protective structures, they largely function as a visible marker of wartime conditions. They are not required everywhere, and there are currently no standards regulating their size or capacity. As an architect who appreciates brutalist concrete forms, I feel that these structures remain visually unresolved, and adding murals would not improve them. It is strange that, at the same time, glass is returning to the city. Glass bus shelters are being rebuilt, façades are being repaired, and even the popular Glass Bridge, which was hit by a missile in May 2023, had its transparent panels replaced within a month. There is something defiant about how quickly the glass returns, as if the city is refusing to let damage dictate its appearance. However, in areas where explosions occur repeatedly, glass is replaced by OSB panels, which cover shattered openings quickly and without much fuss.

Built at the height of the Cold War, the Kyiv metro was designed to function as an effective shelter in the event of a nuclear strike, with all the necessary infrastructure in place. Located deep underground, it is equipped with protective locks and drinking fountains—features that remained undiscovered until 2022. During air-raid alerts, the underground section of the metro is open and free to use. In the event of ballistic missile strikes, having access to a shelter like this provides real comfort. Depending on the situation, some Kyiv residents come to the metro in advance to spend the night, bringing their pets, folding chairs and basic supplies.

Yet there is one problem: the city has grown significantly since the metro was designed, meaning many districts are no longer within reach of a deep station. Furthermore, the river divides the city in two, and the bridges that connect the two halves are strategic targets. During alarms, the bridges are closed. In many newer districts, including those on the left bank, parking structures—either built-in garages or underground car parks—serve as the primary shelters. Various basements, including those of bars and offices, also remain open during air-raid alerts.

However, most of the city's residents stay home. Alongside taping their windows, many people rely on the 'law of probability' (the idea that, statistically, the chance of any single apartment being hit in a large city is low). They also follow the 'law of two walls': according to this theory, it is safest to be deep inside the building, usually in a corridor or bathroom, where the exterior wall and one or two interior walls can soften a blast or stop shrapnel. The level of protection offered varies depending on the building and the nature of the strike, but a corridor provides greater protection than a room with windows. After too many sleepless nights, people often resort to wearing earplugs or headphones, completely ignoring safety precautions.

Clearly, this war is unlike anything we have seen in films. The front line is no longer a single boundary, but rather an area of uncertainty—a kill zone several kilometers deep. How people respond to an alarm often depends on their understanding of the type of strike that may be underway. There are many possibilities:

a confirmed ballistic missile threat, an aircraft taking
off, a salvo of cruise missiles or the detection of strike
and reconnaissance drones. In front line or border
regions, this range of threats is even broader.

As I write this, a major attack on the energy infrastructure has left both electricity and water services out
of action. The metro stopped running on the left bank.

The media reports underground stations and backup
batteries. News programmes show concrete CHPs[1]
wrapped in nets and metal bracing, an image intended
to convey a sense of preparedness. Yet, above ground,
the stations in Kyiv look much the same. Power is sup-
plied according to a schedule, sometimes for only a few
hours a day. All businesses run on generators, and their
low hum fills the streets with noise during blackouts. In
the evening, the streetlights remain dark and the houses
stand unlit, like rocks. People buy batteries of all capaci-
ties to power appliances and refrigerators, or even entire
apartments. They install inverters and solar panels. They
run optical internet cables and attach backup batteries
to their routers. Over the past twenty years, the average
height of new residential buildings has increased to
thirty storeys. However, when the power is out, the
elevators do not work.

Memory and Memorialization

As the war enters its fourth year, new monuments and
practices of remembrance have begun to appear.
Many of them are folk-made, while others are created
by local administrations.

First, flags appeared in cemeteries, placed on the
graves of those who died on the frontlines. Fluttering in
the wind, they altered the stillness of the cemetery. In
the village of Moshchun near Kyiv, the memorial consists

of portraits of the deceased mounted on charred pine tree trunks. An audio recording quietly repeats the names of soldiers who died defending the village. Elsewhere, local administrations turned to quick murals.

In 2023, the public was confronted with another memorial: A photorealistic plastic figure dedicated to a fallen soldier whose execution in captivity had been recorded by Russian forces. Its life-like appearance is unsettling. The most symbolic memorial, however, was improvised on Kyiv's Independence Square. It started with just a few flags on the lawn and gradually spread across the square. Farewells for people who had not followed church traditions, who had not held important public roles, were also held here. Among those honored were Dmitry Kotsiubaylo, commander of the "Da Vinci Wolves" battalion; Shura Ryazantseva; and Davyd Chychkan, an anarchist artist whose work accompanies this publication.

This latest form of public mourning, complete with music, flowers, and smoke bombs, has become a new Ukrainian tradition. It is perhaps more important than monuments, expanding the long-established practice of gatherings and demonstrations in public squares.

In recent months, observing a minute of silence has become routine in public spaces. The announcements and beeping have become another element of Ukraine's auditory landscape, alongside the howling of sirens. People stand up on fast trains and at intersections, while cars stop in the city center.

The Housing Market

Realtors are the most optimistic group in society. They view every news story, official statement or minor change as a potential sign of stability and a potential increase in rental prices.

Prices fell in February 2022 and many contracts were cancelled. Although Kyiv is the capital of Ukraine, there is no support system for internally displaced persons (IDPs). Such centres exist in every regional city, but not here. According to the Deputy Minister of Community and Territorial Development, as of October 25, more than 400,000 IDPs were living in Kyiv, one of the highest numbers in the country. However, the volume of housing being built in Kyiv is now three times lower than last year, with only a third of this falling under the state's affordable housing loan programme, which allows Ukrainians to purchase apartments with preferential mortgage rates ranging from 3 percent for military personnel to 7 percent for IDPs.

There have been many waves of internal displacement over the past ten years due to the occupation, and its subsequent spread of hostility. Those in higher-paid jobs often relocate to Kyiv, which pushes prices up. Another factor is statistical unevenness: Some areas are shelled more frequently and are therefore more dangerous. This includes areas such as the Solomiansky district and the Lukyanivska metro area, where large military production facilities are located. While there may be more rental options for housing or office spaces in these neighbourhoods, one must be prepared to occasionally replace broken windows.

Block Posts and Protests

Checkpoints control the main roads leading in and out of the city. The police conduct random document and cargo inspections there, and similar checks are carried out at railway station entrances. As the railway operates at night, it has become the main method of transport. A curfew is in effect from midnight to 5 a.m., during

which time movement without special permission
is prohibited.

At the beginning of the invasion, there were many
improvised checkpoints throughout the country, set
up in a moment of panic. Every community expected
the arrival of a Russian tank column, so anti-tank messages were painted on road signs, and metal barriers
were hastily constructed. The curfew began at 8 p.m,
at that time and sometimes lasted for several days.
Now, checkpoints and curfews feel more like a formal
procedure to maintain social discipline. This exists
alongside the banning of rallies. Protesting, however,
appears to have become part of Ukrainian public
identity. Following the passing of several controversial
bills in the summer and fall—limiting the independence
of anti-corruption bodies and increasing penalties for
ordinary military personnel—a series of unannounced
rallies took place.

The main political gathering point became the
square near the Franko Theatre, which offered the
clearest view of the Presidential Administration
building. Rallies were even held in front of Parliament,
one of the most tightly controlled areas of the
government quarter.

Many of those driving this new protest culture
were children during the 2013–14 Maidan protests.
They developed a new language of demonstration:
quirky, ironic and meme-like statements on cardboard
signs that merged reality with internet culture.

Appearance of Normalcy

In general, the urban fabric has changed only gradually. After spending the night in a shelter, people
either go to work, or work from home. Some men stay

indoors for fear of being conscripted on the street, while others deliver groceries to them, and still others mobilize voluntarily.

Nowadays, the army offers a wide range of employment opportunities, including roles such as barber, chef, video editors, and programmer. Due to the large number of non-military personnel, the army has become another market sector, complete with competition and a complex structure. Many people work in fields that combine military service with freelance work. Several small miltech start-ups producing drones and radio electronics have emerged. Other companies focus on rapidly deployable modular homes, adaptive renovation solutions or 3D printing for quick reconstruction of critical infrastructure.

Lessons for the Future

In an era where absurd wars can erupt without warning, overturning familiar rules, the question arises: what urban lessons should cities learn? While I was in Graz, Austria in 2022, where my daughter was born, residents of a local housing complex discussed how to prepare for a blackout. Some installed solar panels on their terraces. At the time, this seemed overly cautious to me. Now, however, it feels insufficient.

One of the first priorities should be to safeguard infrastructure by establishing independent electricity, heating, and water networks. Fire safety is equally important, as many people die in fires caused by impacts rather than from the impacts themselves. Construction quality matters too. While it is impossible to build perfect shelters, it is worth analyzing buildings and structures, and creating plans for how ground floors or large interior spaces could be quickly converted into shelters.

Having observed the effects of drone and missile strikes many times, it is clear how different structural systems respond to destruction. A consistent plan for managing these risks would protect residents and strengthen trust in governing institutions and the country as a whole.

If Ukraine survives this war, it will need to change its priorities regarding the built environment. Rather than focusing on appearance or representation, we should prioritize human and environmental safety. Another essential principle should be accessibility, meaning physical conditions that enable everyone, including those without arms, legs or sight, to use public spaces.

Society is struggling to cope with fear, pain and inconvenience, but Kyiv residents still eat out, attend parties, concerts, theater performances and exhibitions, and gather in cafés and public squares.

Looking to the future, governing bodies shall focus on communal interactions and social infrastructure. Rather than romanticizing the past and glorifying war and heroism, a joint effort to secure the things that make a city truly liveable is needed: respect for all living beings within its boundaries. This will require attention to be paid to both the big and the small, the past and the present ●

1   CHP, or Combined Heat and Power, is a system that simultaneously generates electricity and useful heat from a single fuel source.

Oleksandr Burlaka is an architect and photographer with a focus on urban planning and transformations taking place in Ukraine today.

Special thanks to:
Rouven Brües
Zhenia Dvoretska
Anne König
Fabian Mühlthaler
Mariia Shubchyk

Notes on Living
Reflections on Ukraine Today

Edited by: Max Eulitz
Graphic design: Lorenz Klingebiel
Lithography: Oleksii Novikov
Translation: Yustyna Kravchuk,
Sasha Misiura
Copyediting: Zoë Field
Proofreading: Ames Gerould,
Iryna Nikolaichuk
Printing: Westermann Druck Zwickau
Typeface: ABC Favorit (Dinamo)

Published by
Spector Books Verlagsgesellschaft mbH
Harkortstraße 10
04107 Leipzig
www.spectorbooks.com

Distribution:
Germany, Austria: GVA, Gemeinsame
Verlagsauslieferung Göttingen
GmbH&Co. KG,
www.gva-verlage.de
Switzerland: AVA Verlagsauslieferung AG,
www.ava.ch
France, Belgium: Interart Paris,
www.interart.fr
UK: Central Books Ltd,
www.centralbooks.com
USA, Canada, Central and South
America, Africa: ARTBOOK/ D.A.P.,
www.artbook.com
Japan: twelvebooks,
www.twelve-books.com
South Korea: The Book Society,
www.thebooksociety.org
Australia, New Zealand:
Perimeter Distribution,
www.perimeterdistribution.com

First edition: 2026

Printed in the EU

ISBN 978-3-95905-950-3

Image Captions

Marharyta Polovinko (1994–2025)

Page 13, from the series
"Angels 502," 2023,
paper and pencil

Page 22, *No title* (detail),
c. 2022–23, blood on paper

Page 36, from the series
"Angels 502," 2023,
paper and pencil

Page 45, *No title*, 2022,
blood on paper

Page 60, *No title*, 2022,
blood on paper

Page 77, from the series
"Angels 502" (detail), 2023,
paper and pencil

Page 84, *No title*, 2022,
blood on paper

Page 95, *No title* (detail), 2022,
blood on paper

Page 105, *No title*, 2022,
blood on paper

Page 111, from the series
"Angels 502," 2023, paper
and pencil

Page 116, *No title* (detail), 2022,
blood on paper

Cover, both from the series
"Angels 502," 2023, paper
and pencil

Pages in English section

All works photographed by Viktor Pavlenko.
Courtesy: Marharyta Polovinko Estate

Davyd Chychkan (1986–2025)

Page 14, 25, 39, 47, 78, 87, 98, 109
Untitled (With Ribbons and Flags),
watercolor on paper, 86 × 61 cm,
2022–24

Pages in Ukrainian section

Нотатки про життя
Редактор: Макс Ойліц

За участі

Мар'яни Березовської
Оксани Брюховецької
Олександра Бурлак
Насті Воган
Єлизавети Ланденберґер
Юлії Лейтес
Олексія Мінька
Ніхто
Маргарити Половінко
Юлії Стахівської
Давида Чичкана
Аріни Янович

Передмова

Макс Ойліц

Яким був мій шлях до України? Авжеж, через Росію.

Одного теплого вечора, наприкінці літа 2017 року, я сидів із групою самопроголошених анархістів/-ок навколо багаття в маленькому селі Прямухіно, хтозна-де між Пєтєрбургом і Москвою. Відлюдна земля, де роїлись комарі й лилась дешева випивка.

З нагоди 100-ліття Жовтневої революції однодумці/-иці зібралися на кількаденну конференцію у місці народження Міхаїла Бакуніна — славетного революціонера і засновника анархізму. Подія складалася переважно з марудних, довгих лекцій та нескінченних прогулянок навколишніми пшеничними полями.

Згідно з моїм перекладачем, тема зустрічі звучала як «Анархісти проти анархії та анархізму».

Атмосфера була здебільшого невимушеною. Більшість присутніх знали одні одних. Це була строката група жінок і чоловіків різного віку. Ми ночували разом у покинутій школі. Вдень слухали. Ввечері ми пили й дискутували. Ця зустріч аж ніяк не загрожувала державі, проте дуже схоже зібрання зазнало нападу за рік до цього. Молоді неонацисти, пов'язані з Кремлем, штурмували місце проведення конференції. Зрештою, одна людина втратила око.

Та все ж таки того літа симпозіум зібрався знову. Туди, у Прямухіно, прибули радикальні інтелектуали/-ки, хронічно незгодні, ексцентричні й безнадійні оптимісти/-ки. Люди, яким я дійсно симпатизував, які досі вірили в цю країну всупереч режимним розправам, всупереч вбивствам журналістів/-ок та опозиційних діячів/-ок, всупереч військовим атакам на сусідні держави. У моєму щоденнику за 15 серпня 2017 року написано:

«Навколо вогнища: соціалістичні вірші та бойові анархістські гасла. Поки є такі люди, є й надія для цієї країни».

Сьогодні такої надії у мене вже немає. Навіть знаючи про звірства, вчинені проти українського населення, ніхто в Росії не виходить на вулиці. Нема громадянської непокори, нема протесту, нема відкритого спротиву. Полум'яні революціонери/-ки втекли у вигнання або замовкли, зазнавши поразки. Залишки людського тепла полишили це гігантське крижане тіло.

Річ у тім, що якби завтра принаймні третина російського населення припинила працювати й залишилася вдома, війна могла би закінчитися післязавтра. Натомість байдужість тріумфувала. Здається, що непохитність наявного стану тепер є рушійною силою соціальної активності.

Нинішня Україна виглядає як цілковита протилежність. Тут у всій повноті проявляється багатогранність вільного суспільства. Хоча ця воля обмежена реальністю ворожої облоги, громадяни/-ки з власної ініціативи долучаються до суспільної діяльності. Існують громадський дискурс, демонстрації, свобода слова і свобода преси.

Влітку 2018 року я вперше побував у Києві. Хоча ціллю моєї резиденції у Goethe-Institut було дослідження радянських пам'ятників, я врешті-решт не дотримався цього плану. Я змістив фокус на *живі* місця — пам'ятники плинної форми, бастіони громадської активності. Тож я написав книгу про будівництво техноклубу, який незабаром став культурною інституцією — «К41». Місце живого різноманіття та проявів відкритості, яке зрештою взяло на себе відповідальність і в часи війни.

Не хотілось би надто прикрашати драматичну ситуацію, проте путінська операція, очевидно, не досягла своєї головної мети. Замість пригнобленої колонії під ярмом імперіалістичного режиму Україна досі є незалежною державою з політично ангажованими громадянами/-ками.

Відштовхуючись від цієї тези, ця книжка намагається сформулювати бачення майбутнього через осмислення теперішнього. Адже майбутнє України вирішуватиметься не лише на полі битви. Екстремальні ситуації змушують суспільства до випробувань. Відцентрові сили з усіх сторін розривають їхню внутрішню структуру. Саме тому це важливо, попри поляризацію й напругу, — закласти основу для прогресивного, відкритого суспільства.

Послідовним наступником Бакуніна — як ідейним, так і дієвим — був українець Нестор Махно. Він народився 1888 року та, згідно зі своїм ідеологічним наставником, принаймні тимчасово реалізував те, про що той міг лише мріяти. Серед сум'яття громадянської війни 1919–1923 років він на певний час узяв під контроль значну частину України й запровадив колективний устрій рад, заснованих на анархістських принципах. Окрім зміцнення місцевого самоврядування, сьогодні досі резонують його неприйняття авторитарної держави та спротив військовій диктатурі.

Прогресивне ядро

Графіка Давида Чичкана чітко показує, що ці політичні принципи знову актуальні в умовах імперіалістичної загарбницької війни. Це портрети українських та міжнародних лівих військових — анархістів/-ок та соціалістів/-ок, — які приєдналися до збройного

спротиву російському вторгненню та окупації. Сам Чичкан був анархосиндикалістом та антифашистом. Під час повномасштабного вторгнення він не приймав запрошення міжнародних мистецьких інституцій та відмовлявся навіть ненадовго виїжджати за кордон.

Улітку 2024 року Давид припинив працювати над серією і сам добровільно пішов служити мінометником у 241-й бригаді територіальної оборони. Рік потому, 9 серпня 2025 року, він зазнав смертельного поранення в бою від удару російського FPV-дрона.

В одному зі своїх останніх інтерв'ю він сказав:

«Я добровільно йду в армію, тому що я людина лівих поглядів. Це означає, що я проти ексклюзивності та вважаю, що я такий самий, як селяни, вчителі, пролетарі. Я відмовляюся від своїх привілеїв художника, зокрема можливості подорожувати за кордон».

Для нього активна громадська позиція та політична свідомість були невіддільними від мистецької практики.

«Україна — це модерний національний проєкт з лівою та антиавторитарною основою [...] Я вірю, що перемозі неолібералів та неоконсерваторів можна запобігти й повернути сучасну Україну до проєкту, який започаткували українські модерністи/-ки. [...] Україна — це прогресивний проєкт за своєю суттю, цей проєкт опирається пригнобленню».

Зовнішні структури

Такий проєкт модернізації також неминуче обговорюється в полі архітектури. У своєму «Міському путівнику воєнного часу» архітектор і фотограф Майдану Олександр Бурлака (ст. 110) описує, як міські структури адаптуються до війни та які виклики постануть перед мешканцями/-ками міста, коли війна завершиться. Він також розглядає похорон Давида Чичкана як зразок нових форм культури пам'яті.

Київська архітекторка Аріна Янович (ст. 80) обирає подібну далекоглядну перспективу. У своєму тексті вона звертається до київської гаражної культури — спільних просторів, народжених у сотнях міських автогаражів. Це східноєвропейське досягнення може слугувати мікрокосмом і моделлю міського суспільства загалом — за межами капіталістичних імперативів. Після бурхливого будівельного буму 1990-х, коли приватні забудовники були рушійною силою міського розвитку, вона закликає до чітких регуляцій у міському плануванні та пріоритизації солідарності у повсякденному житті. Крізь призму прагматизму вона бачить орієнтири успішної спільноти, для якої інтереси класу забудовників є другорядними на тлі потреб мешканців/-ок міста.

Міжособистісні мережі здатні працювати лише за наявності спільної мови. Тож не дивно, що мовна політика сьогодні для багатьох українців/-ок є гарячою темою. Задовго до повномасштабного вторгнення мову використовували як засіб здійснення влади, виключення й пригнічення. Мар'яна Березовська (ст. 26) розглядає цю суперечливу тему в своєму есе «Мовне питання».

Самосприйняття української ідентичності та відчуття приналежності до суверенної держави

нерозривно пов'язані з прагненням до асоціації із західними цінностями. Утім, дещо ейфорична спрямованість на Захід після Майдану стала значно стриманішою через відсутню чи аж надто нерішучу підтримку під час війни. Ліза Ланденберґер (ст. 100) намагається з'ясувати, чому так званому Заходу настільки важко надати цій країні безумовну та максимальну підтримку.

Подібну перспективу з викликом пропонує текст, підписаний псевдонімом «Ніхто» (ст. 48). Анонімний автор описує роки роботи в Києві над створенням «третього простору», що виходив би за межі національних і гендерних бінарних опозицій, архітектури, що обумовлювала би свободу й приналежність. Текст критично аналізує, як суперечки щодо автентичності та легітимності вплинули на роботу команди. Ніхто стверджує, що справжня інклюзивність вимагає структурних гарантій і правової бази, а також толерантності до відмінностей. Автор висловлює застереження щодо пасток політики ідентичності та націоналістичних тенденцій.

Внутрішні структури

Переходячи від зовнішньої до внутрішньої перспективи, психотерапевтка психоаналітичної школи Юлія Лейтес (ст. 40) ділиться досвідом терапії з військовими та їхніми сім'ями. Текст супроводжує українського військового та його повторювані сни про неминучу смерть і виживання. Авторка відсилає до поняття автопоезису — форми самозбереження через відступ та відновлення — та показує, яким чином акт сну, прогалина й дистанціювання працюють як захисні паузи задля збереження чуттєвості під час війни.

Олексій Мінько (ст. 88) також звертається до снів у своєму художньо-документальному письмі. У наративному стилі, що нагадує магічний реалізм, переплітаються його особисті досвіди під час окупації рідного міста Бердянська, свідчення друзів і подруг, родичів/-ок та інформаційних агентств. Текст Мінька ілюструє сюрреалістичні умови життя й труднощі, через які доводиться проходити під чужим пануванням.

Перехід до інтроверсії та загостреної чутливості також чітко простежується у творчості поетки Юлії Стахівської (ст. 15, 63, 79, 99). Опубліковані тут вірші засвідчують радикальні зміни свідомості в умовах військової ескалації. Її виразні строфи спонукають нас підсилити свої чуття в безповоротно зміненому світі. Вона закликає нас прорватися крізь шум війни.

Так само суб'єктивно, проте відштовхуючись від повсякденних фактів, українська діджейка Настя Воган (ст. 16) рефлексує над своїм життям між трьома домівками: Одесою, Києвом та Берліном. Із невблаганною увагою до трансгресій і атмосферних нюансів, через свої спостереження в транзитних просторах вона підкреслює, що емпатія і порядність не потребують кордонів, а індивідуальна свобода має більшу вагу тоді, коли стає спільною цінністю. Художниця Маргарита Половінко, вочевидь, поділяла це абсолютне уявлення про свободу. Дивлячись на її незабутні малюнки, ми постаємо перед жахами рукотворного пекла. Вона виносить вирок нинішньому *conditio humana*, застосовуючи неконвенційні матеріали на кшталт власної крові чи майже висохлої кулькової ручки, щоб викарбувати на папері зображення, які засвідчують нестерпність ситуації.

Після того як спалахнула війна, Половінко була волонтеркою у Миколаївській та Херсонській областях, де допомагала відбудовувати домівки, зруйновані російськими бомбами. Пізніше вона працювала у складі команди CASEVAC, відповідальної за медичну евакуацію під обстрілами.

В інтерв'ю у листопаді 2023 року вона сказала:

«Зазвичай мистецтво існує там, де складно без нього. З війною мистецтва в моєму житті стало більше. Водночас з'явилось розуміння, що з цим мистецтвом я нічого не можу зробити. Я не можу його ні продати, ні подарувати, бо це кров, це біль, це страждання. Це такий матеріал, для якого немає місця, мені не хочеться, щоб воно існувало. Воно цінне зараз тим, що працює як дзеркало реальності, але я хочу, щоб настав момент, коли воно перестане відображати цей світ».

Восени 2024 року вона зрештою приєдналася до 2-го механізованого батальйону 3-ї окремої штурмової бригади, де служила операторкою дронів. Маргарита загинула на передовій під час виконання бойового завдання 5 квітня 2025 року.

Використання крові як художнього медіуму в роботах Маргарити Половінко аналізує Оксана Брюховецька (ст. 64) в есе «Про кров і найрадикальніший жест турботи». У ньому вона зосереджується на кількох мистецьких практиках у Києві, кожна з яких унікальним чином висвітлює особисті та політичні кризи й зокрема привертає увагу до жіночих артпросторів і квартирних виставок як безпечних просторів у сфері культури.

Свобода України здобувається дорогою ціною. Так було завжди. Нестор Махно боровся за українську автономію все своє життя. Для нього боротьба проти «русского мира» — уявлення про «Велику Росію» — була битвою проти імперіалістичних амбіцій як за царського, так і за більшовицького панування. А незалежна думка та дія — це те, чого імперіалістичні й автократичні режими бояться найбільше. 1934 року, незадовго до своєї смерті у французькому екзилі, Махно написав:

«Свобода кожного індивіда містить у собі зерно вільного суспільства» ●

Макс Ойліц — художник і письменник, що мешкає в Берліні. У 2022 році він опублікував «Notes on 41» — збірку есеїв, що ілюструють обставини створення нічного клубу в Києві.

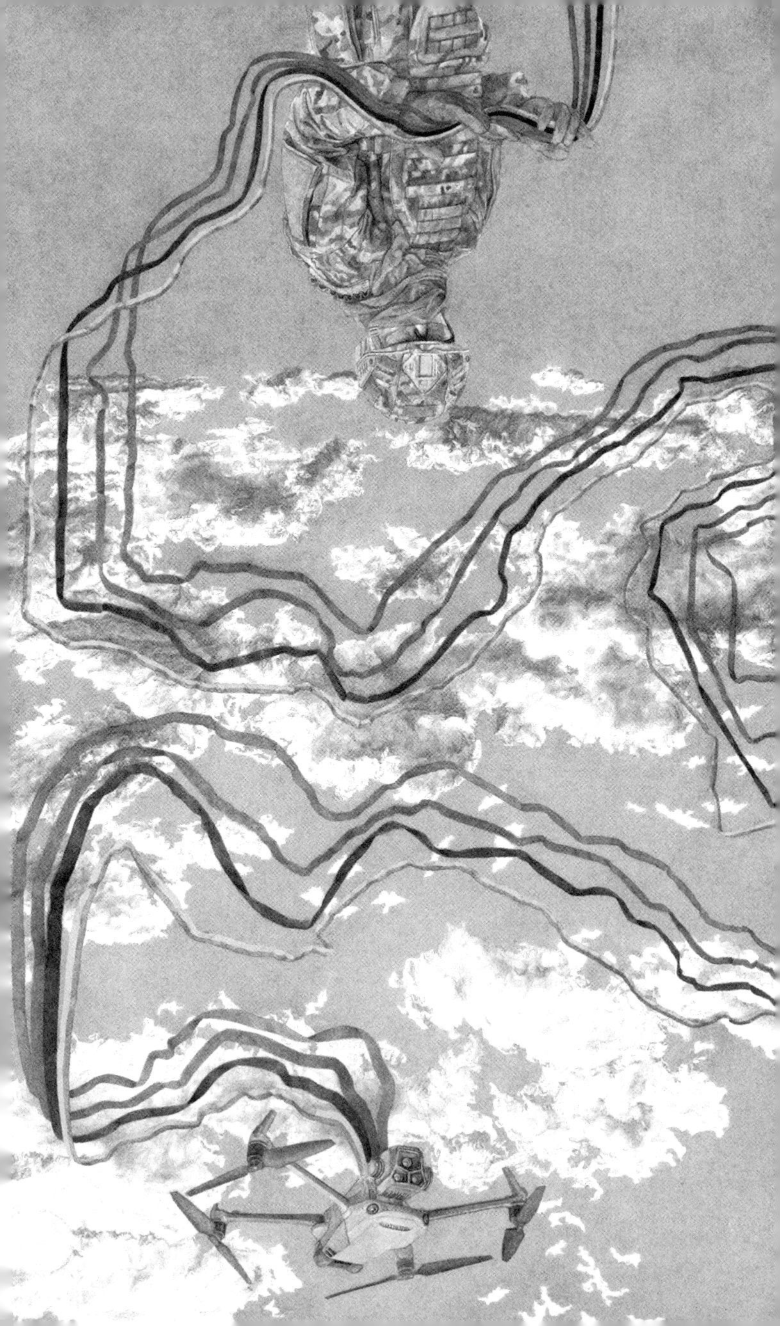

Ніч лагідна

Ніч підбита жовтим атласом ліхтарів.
Їх поставили на місці старих дерев,
і тепер можна подумати:
це і є їх потойбічне життя —
переганяти соки струмів,
зрідка поскрипувати
і збирати навколо комашню,
з розгону вдарятися світляним шершнем у наші
    зелені вікна
і падати на підвіконня ледь живим.

Уночі всі тіла нарощують перламутр
і тужавіють,
щоб заховатися у скойці, мов у труні.

День подібний до мілководдя із пустими
    черепашками на піску.

Юлія Стахівська, 2015

Пункти призначення

Настя Воган

Гортаючи свої нотатки, я пишу ці слова, огорнута стишеною безпечністю мого другого дому — Берліна. Кімната мовчазна й сонлива. Мій власний стан за останні тижні дрейфував у напрямку такого ж спокою. Мабуть це запізніла плата за недавно пережиту інтенсивність у моєму першому домі — Україні. Кожна подорож по-своєму допомагає підтримувати з ним зв'язок.

Через російські повітряні удари й зруйновані повітряні мости Україна потрапила в інший вимір глобального геотемпорального поля. Те, що колись було непомітним півторагодинним авіарейсом, тепер займає понад двадцять чотири години пересадок з одного потяга в наступний — стільки ж часу займає подорож до Тасманії. Змінилася не відстань, а лише архітектура маршруту: об'їзди, затримки та переспрямований повітряний простір. Тіло вивчає цю нову віддаленість у залах очікування та чергах перед контролем безпеки, через повільне накопичення годин, що проходять на шляху до фінальної точки на мапі.

Рух між цими двома місцями ніколи не здається лінійним. Він більше схожий на проникнення крізь мембрану, сплавляння зонами різного тиску. Подорож стає не просто маршрутом, а станом — світ звужується до залізничних коридорів, прикордонних вогнів, перегрітих купе та м'яких вібрацій. Це топологія руху, в якій центр ваги мого тіла зміщується після кожної ледь помітної зміни напрямку. У цьому проміжному просторі поняття від'їзду й вкоріненості припиняють бути протилежностями та натомість стають проявами спільної основоположної тенденції.

Практики свободи

Я глибоко ціную свій привілей — можливість проживати і тут, і там. Утім, моєю здатністю вільно пересуватися між країнами володіють не всі. Або це забороняють чинні закони, або ж вони самі не можуть себе відпустити. Невидимі магніти притягують людей до певних місць.

Друзі-волонтери, які займаються евакуацією з прифронтових територій, розповідали мені про психологічний феномен, коли мешканці відмовляються покидати їхні зруйновані домівки, мотивуючи це тим, що їм потрібно поливати квітник. Квітучі українські сади, доглянуті бабусями, повні чорнобривців і мальв.

Жодна сучасна держава в недавній історії так довго не переживала тривалу катастрофу, продовжуючи при цьому повноцінно функціонувати. В Україні війна проникає в ранкову рутину. Суспільство працює, навчається, творить і кохає — усе під час регулярних атак.

Тож коли щоденна конфронтація з руйнуванням стає звичним тлом, захисні механізми психіки доходять до крайнощів.

Якщо людина не здатна сповна осягнути навіть одну смерть, то як нам упоратися з множинними смертями? Смерть, здається, завжди близько — як думка, як ймовірність, як явище. І цьому немає кінця.

Однак простору для рефлексії над тим, що досі триває, майже нема. Російські дрони й ракетні удари продовжуються і стають ще винахідливішими.

Підозрюю, що тіло зберігає точніші свідчення про війну, ніж пам'ять. Воно згадує кожну повітряну атаку як стискання під ребрами, кожне вимикання

світла як тимчасову сліпоту і втрату контролю і кожен від'їзд як зміну частоти пульсу — особистий архів мікронапружень.

Засинаючи, рахуючи дрони

Кожної ночі в Києві я засинаю з кулоном на шиї. Це два металеві жетони з клубного[1] гардеробу на ланцюжку. На одному з них номер 2666, на іншому — символ ☧. Так моє тіло зможуть ідентифікувати, якщо ракета прилетить у мій дім. Імовірність низька, але не нульова. Цей жетон був подарунком, автор дизайну — мій друг. Так він став клейнодом[2] мого резиденства.

Теплий ланцюжок і кулон на моїй шкірі нагадує мені про власну смертність. Ритуал стає інфраструктурою близькості зі смертю, яка є неминучою і яку неможливо ігнорувати. Кожна прив'язаність є репетицією зникнення — між лібідо і мортидо немає чіткої межі: одне проникає в інше, як тепло в метал. Чи можна по-справжньому зрозуміти цей момент, не переживши його?

Є специфічна властивість в екзистенційних роздумах людей, які проводять ночі, слухаючи вибухи у небі. Під час повітряної тривоги дивні думки починають приходити в голову. Особливо коли ти сама. Коли не можеш заснути перед тим, як усе починається, або прокидаєшся від гуркоту. «Це час у вашому житті, коли ви ставите собі низку запитань: чи задоволені ви тим, хто ви є? Чи просто живете?».[3]

Вибухи. Один, два. Три. Їхній ритм непевний і розладнаний.

Можна пом'якшити гостроту за допомогою теплої істоти, наприклад кота або сусіда.

Кажуть, що діаманти створює тиск.

Чуттєва інфраструктура

Вражає те, як руйнуються зв'язки. Замість того щоб об'єднуватися навколо спільних цінностей, ми часто розділяємося через наші розбіжності, визначаючи себе на противагу тому, на що не хочемо бути схожими.

У підлітковому віці мене лякала думка про те, що люди ніколи не зможуть по-справжньому одне одного зрозуміти. Оскільки емпатія зазвичай базується на спільному досвіді, неможливо сприймати речі однаково, якщо його немає. Тож трансформувати його задля порозуміння неможливо. Можна бачити кольори по-різному, але називати їх однаково. Чи означає це, що суспільство — це насамперед сузір'я поодиноких всесвітів, що ніколи не сходяться, як писав Олдос Гакслі[4]? Чи важливо, що ми бачимо колір однаково, якщо обоє вважаємо його своїм улюбленим?

Сьогодні говорять про глобальну епідемію самотності, тоді як згуртованість стала обмеженим ресурсом, розподіленим нерівномірно, як електрика у час війни.

Іноді я розглядаю внутрішнє тепло як нестійку інфраструктуру, як ненадійну електромережу. Люди носять у собі тремтячі генератори, енергії яких достатньо, щоб обігріти кімнату, телефонний дзвінок, спогад. А що як ця реальна інфраструктура, яку ми несвідомо розбудовуємо, — чуттєва мережа уваги, турботи й нагадувань, маленьких маячків, що нас об'єднують — розпадеться?

Рідні місця

Велика хмара пливе в мій вік. Тату, у нас війна! Уявляєш?

Я у нашому порожньому сімейному будинку в Одесі вперше за чотири роки. Я приголомшена південним затишком навколо.

Моє тепле місто, моя люба троянда, ніжна крапка на мапі. Я бачу протитанкові їжаки та жінок у мерехтливих купальниках на пляжі. Деякі речі не змінюються. Морська вода досі залишає солоні сліди на шкірі, що швидко висихають на сонці. Живі тіла на пляжі сяють темною засмагою, сіллю і світлом, а за кілька кілометрів від них мертве море Куяльника продовжує висихати. Воно здається священнішим за будь-який храм, але навіть екологічний ландшафт стає жертвою цієї війни. Ще один одеський діамант тьмяніє.

Я віддаляюся, але від'їжджати було значно легше, коли дім асоціювався з безпекою.

Проте поняття дому постійно змінюється — розширюється, скорочується, розчиняється. Одеса, Київ, Берлін — у кожному з цих місць є щось особливе, і жодне з них не викреслює інше. Спочатку я думала, що в мене один дім, потім — два, але тепер це сукупність місць, які борються за мене навіть тоді, коли я вже повністю їм не належу. Можливо, тому рух приносить біль — адже кожне прибуття є також маленькою зрадою іншого місця.

Внутрішні кордони

У цьому розширеному способі життя я продовжую вивчати нову фізику кордонів. Я дізнаюся, які з них дозволяють тілу пройти без питань, які зустрічають стримано та які імітують ніжність, приховуючи за собою гострий кут.

У берлінському Кройцберґу я сиджу на березі Ландвер-каналу, що виблискує, залитий променями

вечірнього сонця. З'являється поліцейський катер і урочисто пливе до мене. Він пропливає повз, а за ним п'ять-шість менших каяків. «Свобода пересування — право кожного!» — кричить протестувальник/-ця у гучномовець. Інші демонстранти/-ки пропливають повз, скандуючи: «Ні кордонів, ні націй! Припиніть депортації!».

Їхні голоси вілунюють від води і розчиняються у вітрі. Усе це виглядає щиро й дивно, трохи недоречно, наче якась танцювальна сцена у фільмі. Я дивлюся і думаю про всіх, кому доводилося проходити через кордон проти їхньої волі. Думаю про кордони, які припиняють бути метафорою, коли їх розтоптує чужа армія. «Поважайте мої кордони», — думаю я.

Протестувальники/-ці на човнах скандують: «Нехай впаде фортеця Європа!». Я стискаюся, думаючи про своїх друзів і подруг, які захищають мої кордони, свободу і права. У них немає іншого вибору, але вони все одно мусять робити цей вибір. Де закінчуються стіни європейської фортеці? Як ці добрі люди можуть бути такими байдужими? Водночас я рада, що вони можуть висловитися, зважаючи на те, що попередні покоління вибороли для них таку можливість.

10999

Я знову повертаюся з Києва, вкрита пилом подорожі, запахами дизельного палива, розчинної кави та чужих парфумів. Моя шкіра липка від двадцяти шести годин у дорозі. Потяги здаються тимчасовими, трохи занедбаними будинками на колесах. Іноді провідники прикрашають їх дивними, ніби язичницькими, ритуальними об'єктами. Одного разу в поїзді, у вузькій сірій вбиральні з металевими стінами,

я нарахувала двадцять два декоративні ароматичні мішечки, розставлені як обереги. Вагон стає лоном, коридором переходу, камерою, де ідентичності згладжуються. Я не припиняла думати про людину, яка їх розмістила — наскільки сильним мало бути її бажання створити відчуття дому всередині чогось, що ніколи не зупиняється.

Потяг Варшава—Берлін запізнювався. Під час такої довгої подорожі додаткові години проходять удвічі довше. Основна затримка відбулася у Львові, де збивали дрони, що прямували в Європу.

Київ здається напруженим і наелектризованим, із золотисто-помаранчевими відтінками, що просвічують крізь метал, налаштовуючись на тон неминучої небезпеки. Натомість Берлін — пористий і сонний. Це тьмяно освітлене місце для рефлексій. Вулиці освітлені слабо. Його сумнозвісні сутінки можна розглядати як безперервну репетицію блекауту.

Вдома, у моєму нібито безпечному місці, почуваюся незвично, наче воно пам'ятає стару версію мене. Я знімаю кулон і нарешті засинаю. Наступного ранку я прокидаюся від звуку сирен.

Це була пробна тривога. Втім, берлінським сиренам бракує тієї розривної ноти відчаю — глибини невідкладності, людського крику в інтонації. Вони не справляють на мене великого враження. Я продовжую запитувати, чи може емпатія прокинутися без звуку сирен ●

Настя Воган — українська діджейка, що мешкає в Берліні.

1   К41 (також ∄ або Кирилівська 41) — нічний клуб на Подолі у Києві.

2   Символічні атрибути військової або цивільної влади, зокрема
     в українських козаків у XV–XVIII ст.

3   Цитата з Underground Resistance: Transition / Windchime, Released:
     2002, US.

4   О. Гакслі «Брама сприйняття»: «Ми проводимо життя разом, діємо
     спільно і взаємопов'язані одне з одним; але завжди і за всіх обста-
     вин залишаємося наодинці із собою. Мученики входять на арену
     тримаючись за руки, але тортури зазнають кожен наодинці. Коханці
     несамовито прагнуть злити в обіймах свої відокремлені пори-
     вання почуттів у єдине самопіднесення — марно. За самою своєю
     природою кожен утілений дух приречений страждати й радіти на
     самоті». (Переклад О. Буценка, 1994).

Мовне питання

Мар'яна Березовська

Десятиліттями Росія використовувала той факт, що багато українців/-ок розмовляють російською, аби стверджувати, що ми «один народ». Росія тривалий час використовувала мову як інструмент заперечення української ідентичності й виправдання політичного панування. Я часто думаю, наскільки абсурдною здалася б ця логіка в інших багатомовних країнах на кшталт Бельгії чи Швейцарії, де спільна із сусідньою державою офіційна мова ніколи не використовувалась, щоб поставити під сумнів їхню «справжність» або проголосити, що їхні громадяни/-ки потребують порятунку. А втім, саме цей аргумент став зброєю щодо України. Як тільки виникає ймовірність надання російській хоч якогось офіційного статусу, російські пропагандисти миттєво використовують це як доказ того, що Україна «належить» Росії.

Дуже простим і водночас потужним жестом опору є, власне, розмовляти українською. Наша мова завжди була політизованою, але тепер вона набуває нового значення: це спосіб домогтися свого, говорити за себе зсередини країни, а не з екзилю. Це рідкісний момент у нашій історії, коли, незважаючи на кризу, ми нарешті здобули колективний голос, здатний документувати й визначати, що відбувається — нашою власною мовою, а не через голоси інших.

Протягом століть інтелектуали Російської імперії зневажали українську як мову селян — щось фольклорне й емоційне, проте аж ніяк не інтелектуальне. Більшість витончених українських літературних творів, праць із філософії та лінгвістики, які спростовували це уявлення, писалися підпільно або в екзилі. Тривалий час наша культура виживала за межами країни завдяки тим, хто був змушений її покинути.

Сам по собі цей досвід не був унікальним. По всій Європі під час формування національних держав мова була головним полем битви: ідентичності утверджували, узгоджували й заперечували через мову, й багато новоутворених держав були змушені боротися за право розмовляти й писати власною мовою. Однак у випадку України ця боротьба була систематичною й тривалою. Українських письменників/-ць та мислителів/-ок, які наполягали на використанні власної мови, цензурували, обмежували й позбавляли права публікуватися. Багатьом доводилося навчатися, працювати й видаватися в межах Російської імперії, де зосереджувалась інституційна та економічна підтирмка, а українська культурна автономія водночас активно придушувалась.

Російська імперія послідовно відмовляла Україні в умовах для вільного культурного та лінгвістичного розвитку. Історично Україну розглядали як простір бунту та спротиву — територію, яку варто контролювати замість надати їй право незалежно висловлюватись. Ця динаміка тривала не десятиліттями, а століттями — і ми досі живемо в епіцентрі цієї боротьби.

Проте зараз ми проживаємо рідкісний і винятковий момент в українській історії, коли ця інтелектуальна і творча енергія має простір для існування радше у межах країни, ніж у вигнанні за кордоном. Водночас дискусія навколо мови досі напружена: це розрив між поколіннями, між регіонами, між людьми. Та дедалі більше людей переходять на українську — не лише починають нею говорити, а й мислити, — і я хочу дослідити, що означає цей зсув.

В мені є частка російської ідентичності — не суттєва чи домінантна, тому що я ніколи насправді не мала зв'язку зі своїм батьком-росіянином. Але

я досі чітко пам'ятаю, як до семи років проводила літо у Пскові. За літо я переходила на російську, і після повернення додому в Луцьк мені потрібен був час, аби знову переключитися на українську. Востаннє я була у Пскові ще дитиною — мама відвозила мене туди двадцятичотиригодинним потягом із Луцька. Моя українська бабуся забирала мене в кінці літа, і я досі пам'ятаю, як вона казала, що не гратиметься зі мною, поки я не перейду назад на українську. Вона називала мене «мале кацапеня». Трохи згодом поїзд скасували. Моя мама припинила відвозити мене до дідуся й бабусі.

Я пам'ятаю реакції вихователейок на російські слова, що прокрадалися в мою мову після повернення із цих подорожей. Одного разу нам треба було підібрати слова на літеру А. Я сказала «арбуз». Мене виправили на «гарбуз», але сама я відразу подумала: ні, йдеться ж про кавун. Навіть тоді у мене було певне лінгвістичне усвідомлення — відчуття, що слова є не просто словами. Вони мають вагу. Вони мають походження. Вони із чимось пов'язані. Тепер, коли мені відомі поняття на кшталт «деколонізованого мислення» й «інтерсекційності», здається, що вони тут можуть дещо пояснити. Проте я не знала їх, коли мені було шість років.

У ХХ столітті українське інтелектуальне письмо про українську мову існувало переважно в екзилі. Центр наших лінгвістичних досліджень — роботи, яка сформувала наше розуміння історії, структури та філософії української мови — був створений за кордоном, за межами країни, мову якої він прагнув захистити. Найочевиднішим прикладом тут є робота Юрія Шевельова. Один із найважливіших українських лінгвістів, літературних критиків та істориків

мови покинув Харків під час Другої світової війни та провів решту життя у Сполучених Штатах. Усі його провідні праці — від «Історичної фонології української мови» до есеїв про українську ідентичність — були написані далеко від України, серед діаспори, що намагалася зберегти українську культуру, коли радянська держава репресувала її вдома. Це було закономірністю протягом поколінь: українська інтелектуальна думка виживала в Нью-Йорку, Мюнхені, Торонто, але рідко у Києві чи Харкові.

Аж ось, раптом, ми живемо у час, коли українською можна писати, розвивати її, теоретизувати та збагачувати всередині країни. Коли люди пишуть українською з Києва, Львова, Харкова, Одеси — не з вигнання. Здається, що вперше в нашій сучасній історії ми не лише зберігаємо нашу мову, а й розширюємо її зсередини. Цей момент варто захищати й плекати, тому що він крихкий і безпрецедентний — шанс, якого в попередніх поколінь українських мислителів/-ьок просто не було.

На початку 2010-х я вивчала лінгвістику в Національному лінгвістичному університеті у Києві. Багато моїх одногрупників/-ць були із заходу України — не з великих міст, як Львів чи Івано-Франківськ, а з маленьких містечок та сіл. Я помічала у багатьох із них певний комплекс меншовартості. Як тільки вони прибували у Київ та виходили за межі нашого гуртожитка, особливо якщо влаштовувались десь на студентську роботу, вони переходили на російську. Існував тиск — справжній структурний тиск. Якщо не перейти, то тебе могли таврувати як «село». Я ніколи не переходила, але відчувала це: у громадському транспорті, магазинах, запитуючи дорогу на вулиці.

На першому році навчання у нас була викладачка ділової української мови — відома лінгвістка, яка тоді навіть навчала Юлію Тимошенко розмовляти українською (стільки мемів спадають на думку, поки я це пишу). На одній із перших пар вона у зверхньому тоні сказала: «Тут ми не кажемо «тудою-сюдою»[1]. Так говорять у селі, з якого ви приїхали».

Мене шокувало відкриття того, що ці слова «заборонені». Ці українські еквіваленти англійських *hereby/thereby* або німецьких *dort lang/hier lang* були настільки корисні, що я не могла зрозуміти, чому їх витіснили з мовної норми.

Пам'ятаю, як поверталася в рідне місто і змушувала маму також припинити вживати ці слова, щоб не звучати як «село», і замість них казати «цією дорогою, цим шляхом». Значно пізніше, на магістерській програмі з лінгвістики у Потсдамі, я писала дипломну роботу про «мовний престиж»: чому одні мови й акценти стають «престижними», а інші — ні? Яким чином ми формуємо наші враження про людей на основі того, як вони розмовляють, часто зчитуючи авторитет, інтелект або культурну цінність з акценту, хоча мова нічого не каже нам про людський характер та здібності?

Цей феномен детально вивчався в контексті британського варіанту англійської — її колоніальної історії, утисків локальних мов та внутрішньої ієрархії акцентів у межах самої Британії. Існує тривале розуміння того, як англійська, зокрема її престижніші акценти, стала домінувати в місцях, де були свої історичні мови, в яких відібрали умови для повноцінного розвитку та можливості пишатися своєю відмінною лінгвістичною традицією. Ця дискусія оновилася і набула широкого розголосу 2025 року завдяки Кпеесар[2].

Моя дипломна фокусувалася на меншій престижності української порівняно з російською у великих містах та на її історичному контексті — як ключові міста розбудовувались навколо індустрій, як книжки публікувалися переважно російською, як поширювалось нормативне використання російської в системі освіти, як розмовна українська почала зводитися до мови «селян». Наприклад, дуже мало людей знають, що навіть на Донбасі багато сіл досі україномовні. Російськомовними є саме міста. Я навіть розглянула випадок «тудою/сюдою», проте не знайшла достатньо академічних свідчень, щоб пояснити, чому ці практичні слова не ввійшли до норми української мови.

Мовне питання завжди було проблемним. Я завжди пов'язувала його із тим, чому мені не вдалося сповна інтегруватися в Києві у 2010-х — чому я ніколи не почувалася там як удома. Як не дивно, повернувшись у 2025 році з Берліна до Києва, щоб знову жити тут, я опинилася в тому ж районі, де був мій студентський гуртожиток. Місцевість суттєво змінилася — всюди сучасні житлові комплекси, — але вайб залишився той самий.

Я чую на диво багато української в магазинах, метро і на вулиці. Власне кажучи, здебільшого українську. Проте багато підлітків досі розмовляють російською. Навпроти районної адміністрації та місцевої гімназії є великий меморіал з іменами й історіями людей з цієї місцевості, які загинули на війні з 2022 року. Хотілось би, щоб школярі/-ки, проходячи повз меморіал, могли зрозуміти, яке велике значення має українська мова — не як обов'язок, а як усвідомлення того, за що ведеться ця війна, та як ушанування людей, які віддали своє життя, щоб вони могли ходити до школи, рости і жити у вільній Україні.

Я також думаю про тих, кого катували й убивали в російському полоні, де розмовляти українською заборонено — саме тому, що їхні кати її не розуміють. У їхніх життях мова не була абстрактною. Це те, за що людей карали і за що вони трималися навіть тоді.

Але багато людей досі розмовляють так, ніби їх евакуювали з Москви. Мені дуже боляче це чути, тому що я розумію, що не всі проживають цю війну однаково. Як на мене, це надзвичайно сумно, особливо якщо йдеться про нове покоління, яке має далі жити у звільненій Україні.

На перших курсах університету, коли нарешті могла подорожувати самостійно, я двічі поверталася в Росію до своєї бабусі через одинадцять років із часу нашої останньої зустрічі. Пам'ятаю, як останнього разу, коли там була, я чекала на поїзд до Києва у Псковській області на станції під назвою «Дно».

Я сиділа на лавці кілька годин, читаючи «Хозарський словник»³. П'яний чоловік сів біля мене й коментував книжку, оскільки якимось чином знав про Милорада Павича. Його телефон задзвонив ринґтоном однієї з пісень Muse, а потім його забрали мєнти. Мені треба було в туалет, але двері там не зачинялися, тож я терпляче чекала на лавці до прибуття потяга.

В моїй уяві Росія — це саме та станція. Це *дно*. Це *мєнти*. Це п'яні чоловіки, непереконливе прагнення культури та вічні страждання. Деколи мені хотілось би, щоб усі, хто досі розмовляє російською, побували на станції «Дно», щоб побачити, що означає бути Росією і як їм пощастило бути не там.

У шкільні роки в Луцьку я сім років навчалася гри на скрипці. Мій вчитель Ігор Сметанін і його дружина-піаністка були шанованими інтелектуалами в

місті та розмовляли російською мовою. Їхня родина, мабуть, потрапила в Луцьк унаслідок військової передислокації (хтось у сім'ї, ймовірно батько, був військовим, якого туди відправили на службу). Як і всі інші російські сім'ї, з якими часто стикаєшся, вони ніколи не переходили на українську. Вони завжди розмовляли російською з цією неочевидною дистанцією. Наче натякали: «Ми не такі, як ви». Ця прихована відчуженість була завжди присутня, хоча й не обов'язково в агресивній формі.

Моя мама завжди переходила на російську, коли з ними розмовляла. Вона ностальгувала за роками навчання в Росії та «величчю російської культури». Мене це завжди дратувало. Я думала: «Поважай себе, мамо. Не роби цього». І просто продовжувала розмовляти українською.

Їхній син Ілля Сметанін був моїм однолітком й у той самий час навчався гри на скрипці. Він вступив до консерваторії і став відомим скрипалем. Їхня родина завжди мала особливу ауру — вишукану, освічену, вищу за провінційну. Інтелектуальна еліта міста.

Коли 2022 року почалося повномасштабне вторгнення, виявилося, що Ілля був зрадником. Росія завербувала його до 2014 року — під час поїздки до Москви, нібито як одного з тих, кого, за їхніми словами, треба було «рятувати» із західної України. Врешті-решт він почав працювати на російську армію. Він був причетний до удару по військовому аеродрому в моєму рідному місті.

Тепер, після вторгнення, багато моїх друзів перейшли на українську. Мене здивувало, наскільки невимушено це відбулося — наскільки природно вони стали звучати. Мої найближчі тутешні друзі

з Києва та навколишніх містечок, з Донецька та Луганська, Харкова та з Дніпропетровської області — усі колишні затяті російськомовні. Легкість цього переходу мене щиро здивувала.

Я знаю, що деяким із них було важко змінити своє мислення та читацькі звички. У деяких досі напружені стосунки з батьками, які продовжують розмовляти російською. Проте важливо розуміти, що покоління докорінно змінилися, і немає сенсу намагатися переробити тих, хто ностальгує за Радянським Союзом, за своєю молодістю, за праг-неннями того часу. Майбутнє належить людям, які борються у цій війні та які її переживуть. Багато з нас не виживуть.

До українців/-ок за кордоном, які досі розмовля-ють російською, у мене лише одне питання: «Чи не соромно вам, що вас можуть сприйняти як рускіх?».

Я чудово знаю — щодо цього є багато думок. Навіть деякі автори/-ки у цій книзі досі російсько-мовні, і я, відверто кажучи, сумнівалася, чи хочу публікуватися разом з ними. Коли я про це думаю, то усвідомлюю, наскільки зверхньо це звучить і що я не знаю їхніх історій. Колись хотілось би взяти інтерв'ю у людей, які досі розмовляють російською, щоб краще зрозуміти їхню логіку чи принаймні задокументувати це явище.

Я також усвідомлюю, що перебуваю в привілейо-ваній позиції — сиджу на високому (українському) коні й засуджую тих, кому складно говорити укра-їнською. Я із заходу, у мене були прекрасні вчите-лі/-ьки, моя сім'я завжди спілкувалася українською і ніколи не дивилася Соловйова[4]. Двері гаража мого дядька пофарбовані у червоно-чорне[5]. Відверто кажучи, я — ідеальна кандидатура для російської

пропаганди, щоб виправдати вторгнення та так зване «визволення»: мене можна змалювати як «жахливу нацистку», що начебто робить життя росіян/-ок в Україні нестерпним, заперечуючи їхнє право на існування й таким чином зміцнюючи переконання у тому, що російськомовних треба «звільнити» від таких українців/-ок, як я.

Але я також знаю історії, що ускладнюють цю картину, і вони для мене важливі. Це історії друзів і подруг, які переїхали з окупованого Криму й Донбасу до Києва чи за кордон і мусили переосмислити, хто вони. Історії тих, хто роками вірили російській пропаганді, а потім повільно від неї відучувалися — не через гасла чи шкільні підручники, які переписували з кожною зміною уряду, а через особисті зустрічі та життєвий досвід. Історії людей, які перейшли на українську і більше не знаходять спільної мови з батьками. Змішаних сімей, радянських міграцій, ідентичностей, сформованих радше обставинами, ніж власним вибором. Людей, що опираються мовному переходу не через вірність Росії, а через недовіру до української держави або відчуття, що вона їх покинула. Історії меншин в Україні, чиї культури і мови також недостатньо чули або захищали.

Україна велика і надзвичайно складна — країна сорока мільйонів людей до повномасштабного вторгнення, сформована століттями насильства, експлуатації та сум'яття, що суттєво передує появі російського імперіалістичного проєкту, тому жодна окрема історія не може її змалювати[6].

І все ж, поза всіма цими особистими історіями й поза складністю ідентичностей — історіями людей, місцями їхнього походження, тим, як і якою мовою

вони розмовляють, — є одна річ, яку я ношу в собі
і яка здається простою та абсолютною, навіть коли
все інше є багатогранним і заплутаним. У цій війні,
що триває, поки я це пишу, моїм провідником
є голос Катерини Мотрич — акторки й дружини
українського актора та військового Юрія Феліпенка,
вбитого на війні на початку 2025 року. На його
похороні, стоячи над його тілом, вона тремтячим
голосом сказала:

*«Я всіх прошу: убийте в собі все російське.
Саме через Росію ми сьогодні тут — дивимося
на холодне тіло Юри. Забудьте мову ворога.
І мстіться».*

Чого б це не коштувало, ти мусиш убити Росію
у собі, щоб вижити у цій війні. Для мене мова —
один із найпотужніших способів цього досягти.
Це найчіткіший спосіб виразити мою позицію ●

Мар'яна Березовська — письменниця, кураторка та культурна продюсерка, яка працює між Берліном та Києвом. Вона є співзасновницею журналу Borshch та менеджеркою лейблу Standard Deviation.

1   «Тудою» й «сюдою» — історично властиві українській мові слова, зафіксовані в словниках. У сучасній українській вони вважаються розмовними або діалектними, тому їх уникають в офіційній нормі, хоча самі слова залишаються цілком природними і корисними.

2   Kneecap — ірландське хіп-хоп тріо з Белфасту (Північна Ірландія). Колектив виступає за юридичний статус та відродження ірландської мови (*Gaeilge*) в Північній Ірландії — справа з глибоким корінням у спільній історії антиколоніального спротиву та соціально-політичному контексті, що сформувався після Північноірландського конфлікту.

3   «Хозарський словник» (серб. *Хазарски речник / Hazarski rečnik*) — перший роман сербського письменника Милорада Павича, опублікований 1984 року. Я читала його в рамках моєї університетської програми.

4   Владімір Соловйов — російський журналіст і телеведучий, найбільш відомий як ведучий політичних ток-шоу «Вечір з Владіміром Соловйовим» і «Москва. Кремль. Путін» на державному каналі «Росія-1», а також «Соловйов Live». Він є видатною фігурою в державних кремлівських медіа і відвертим прихильником війни Росії проти України, анексії Криму та політики Владіміра Путіна.

5   Червоне й чорне — кольори прапора Української повстанської армії (УПА), пов'язаної з українським визвольним рухом XX століття. Кольори переважно інтерпретують як символ крові, пролитої за визволення й землю.

6   Тим, хто цікавиться ширшим історичним контекстом сучасної України та її відносинами з сусідніми імперіями, я особисто раджу серію лекцій Тімоті Снайдера «Становлення сучасної України» (*The Making of Modern Ukraine*, Yale Courses, YouTube).

Не готові до світла

Юлія Лейтес

Щоразу перед пораненням він бачив його уві сні. Вночі перед тим, як 152-міліметровий снаряд влучив у його позицію, Р. снилося знову:

Він був у літньому саду своєї бабусі — безпечній гавані дитинства, серед кущів бузку та поіржавілих гойдалок. Там стояв сторожовий гном — одна із тих розфарбованих фігурок, яким зазвичай нічого стерегти.

У сні гном із ним заговорив і показав на свіжовикопану могилу. Коли Р. придивився, то зрозумів, що могила не має дна — вона відкривається у чорну діру. Гном звелів йому стрибнути вниз. Р. відмовився. «Не сьогодні, — сказав він. — Мені є що робити. Можеш почекати».

Наступного ранку снаряд влучив прямо в окоп. Вибух пробив стелю, поховавши Р. живцем під колодами й землею. Побратим завдяки якійсь неймовірній інтуїції викопав його до того, як він задихнувся. Його хребет розтрощився, а тіло розкололося під вагою дерев'яних балок бліндажа.

Р. евакуювали спочатку в польовий шпиталь, потім у центральний госпіталь. Морфін проник у його кров — спочатку як ліки, потім як надія. Як і в пісні *Sister Morphine* Маріанни Фейтфулл, межа між зціленням і зникненням затьмарилася.

Пізніше, коли він переповів мені свій сон, я розтлумачила його не як пророцтво, а як психічну репетицію винищення. Такі сни часто навідують військових — передчасні фантазії, що інсценують смерть у просторі сну, щоб тіло наяву могло рухатись далі. Несвідоме нездатне запобігти удару снаряда й натомість намагається його зобразити — вмістити невмістиме.

У психоаналітичній термінології сон і сновидіння — це два різні процеси. Сон — це нічна робота, спрямована на збереження цілісності психіки, на підзарядження тіла. Сновидіння, згідно з Фройдом,— це функція психіки, що захищає сон від бажань і страхів, які майже ніколи не вгамовуються та намагаються нас розбудити, перервавши процес підзарядки. Тож психіка знаходить вихід у формі роботи сновидіння — постійної символізації сирого матеріалу несвідомого в образах, історіях, фрагментах значення. Таким чином, гном виконує роль психопомпи — фігури переходу, позначаючи момент, коли робота сновидіння захищає роботу сну — перетравлюючи жах, коли тіло не може заспокоїтися.

Описаним вище сном зі мною поділився мій клієнт — військовий Збройних Сил України, з яким я розпочала психоаналітичну психотерапію на початку 2023 року. Через півтора року нашої роботи він розповів ще один сон.

Він сидів серед руїн мікрорайону — одного з радянських кварталів на околицях міста з ідентичними панельними будинками, розташованими навколо комунального подвір'я. Посередині знаходився дитячий майданчик: пісочниця, увігнута гірка, каркас гойдалки. Це було десь на сході України — в одному з тих міст, про які чуєш хіба що в новинах, десь біля фронту.

Саме там покоління, яке зростало в замаскованій під комунізм імперії, вперше дізналося, що означає «ми». Це «ми» тепер розкололося на тих, хто досі там, і тих, хто поїхали.

Уві сні Р. сидів на лавці на дитячому майданчику, оточеному напівзруйнованими «панельками». Усе було чорно-біле, німе, неживе.

Раптом він відчув потребу подзвонити мені. Він простягнув руку по телефона у правій кишені штанів. Але коли спробував його дістати, то зрозумів, що всі п'ять пальців його руки зламані. Вони були на місці, але не реагували — так наче більше не підкорялися. Темрява навколо нього згущувалася, коли він відчайдушно намагався набрати мій номер.

Потім зненацька з'явилася лінія світла — тонкий горизонтальний розріз. Він відчув необхідність її перетнути. На іншому боці була вулиця Хрещатик у центрі Києва, сповнена світла і барв у святковий день: сім'ї гуляли, жінки тримали в руках квіти, діти сміялися.

Стоячи там, він подивився вниз і побачив свій одяг — брудний, затверділий від крові й болота з окопів. Запах диму й гниття вп'явся у нього. Світло навколо засліплювало, майже осудливо. Він зрозумів, що йому не місце серед цієї ясності: вона радше робила його беззахисним, ніж зігрівала. І тоді він відчув її — гравітацію темряви, знайому, могутню. Вона затягувала його назад до себе.

Він зробив вибір і ступив назад у пітьму, знову опинившись на зруйнованому майданчику, знову намагаючись набрати мій номер зламаними пальцями.

Тоді він прокинувся.

Після того як Р. розповів мені свій сон, я продовжувала повертатися до цього місця. Дитячий майданчик у центрі мікрорайону, оточений

одноманітними радянськими панельками, колись був архітектурою спільності, образом, що об'єднував покоління.

Тепер, у його сні, цей простір постає монохромним: ні світла, ні кольору — лише відтінки попелу. Колективний простір вижив, проте лише як фотографічний негатив самого себе, залишившись у темній кімнаті психіки — досі вологий, досі тремтливий, ще не готовий проявитися. Не готовий до світла.

Для мене таке відторгнення світла є радше ознакою збереження, ніж негативної регресії. Психіка уникає проміння, наче рана, що закривається від повітря — тимчасова пітьма необхідна для можливості зцілення.

Це те, що я знову і знову бачу в тих, хто не може спати чи остаточно прокинутися, або у тих, хто поїхали, — не уникнення життя, а дивовижний тип відданості йому. Якась частина організму знає, що повинна відступити перед тим, як рухатись далі.

У 1970-х двоє чилійських біологів Умберто Матурана й Франческо Варела запропонували поняття для опису цієї динаміки. Вони назвали її «автопоезис», що походить від грецького αὐτο- (*auto*) — «сам» і ποίησις (*poiesis*) — «створення, виробництво». Живий організм, писали вони, існує не завдяки матерії, з якої складається, а завдяки безперервній роботі самовідновлення. Клітина продовжує жити лише завдяки оновленню мембрани, що відмежовує її від потенційних подразників.

Утім, ця логіка самотворення притаманна не лише клітинам. Згідно з нею живуть і річки. Вони відходять від своїх берегів, розмивають їх, перекроюють їх, завжди виробляючи форму, що зберігає їхнє життя. Коли течія стає надто сильною,

річка згортається, тяжіє всередину, прокладає новий шлях через мул і морок. Вона не припиняє курсувати, а змінює напрямок. Я часто думаю, що психіка працює так само. Коли середовище стає токсичним, вона відступає назад саме настільки, наскільки потрібно, щоб потім продовжити свій потік.

І сон, і від'їзд у певному сенсі є малою й великою версією того самого акту — можливістю регенерації себе, тимчасовим відступом задля шансу виживання.

Коли сон порушується, як це часто буває на війні, ментальна система стає відкритою до бомбардування — і буквального, і психічного, — аж поки не почне руйнуватись. Саме це я бачу у снах військових — не пророцтво, не містику, а відчайдушне збереження буття, невидиму реставрацію, що відбувається в темряві, коли психіка репетирує власну загибель.

Від'їзд спирається на подібну логіку, проте в іншому масштабі. Це не екзиль у класичному чи трагічному сенсі, не «ностос» — жага повернутись додому, — а щось ближче до макросну. Це спосіб психіки приглушити світло, коли вразливість перед реальністю стає нестерпною. Ті, хто залишають Україну чи будь-яке інше місце катастрофи, відмовляються не від приналежності, а від фізичного і психічного знищення. Поїхати — це лише один зі способів збереження здатності відчувати.

Сон, від'їзд, мовчанка — це паузи, через які реальність можна знову помислити. Це повільні акти автопоезису, здійснені психікою, це робота з відтворення межі, тихе промовляння: я досі тут, хоча й поки що мушу побути у темряві.

Водночас кожне відео з дрона, кожна телетрансляція з фронту, кожна зруйнована будівля прагне бути побаченою. Однак психічне життя працює по-іншому, воно не може вижити під постійним впливом подразника. Воно потребує непрозорості, прихованості, закадровості. Може здатися, що це лють проти світла, заперечення істини, утім, я це трактую як сплячку — умову для повернення сенсу.

Навіть у пітьмі пам'ять не припиняє проявлятися. Треба лише знайти спосіб прокинутися, побачити сон, продовжити набирати телефонний номер ●

Юлія Лейтес — психотерапевтка-психоаналітикиня з Києва, Україна, кандидатка Міжнародної психоаналітичної асоціації.

Нотатки з третього простору

Ніхто

2018 року я переїхав до Києва, щоб допомогти створити, як я сподівався, «третій простір» — місце за межами бінарностей національності, гендеру та ієрархій, що формують більшість наших соціальних світів. Простір свободи, де такі цінності могли би проживатися, а не лише обговорюватися. П'ять років я співпрацював над створенням цього простору з українськими колегами, для української публіки, в українському місті, котре саме намагалося визначити, що взагалі означає бути «українським».

Цей текст написаний саме з цієї позиції — глибокої залученості, але й постійної відстороненості, відданості побудові того, що водночас прославляли як символ «нової України» й критикували як щось «нетутешнє». Схвалювали за розвиток міжнародних зв'язків та сприймали з підозрою, тому що їх розвивав аутсайдер. Я жив між Берліном і Києвом, між мовами, між відчуттям, що я ніде не свій, і щоденною роботою над створенням місця, де інші могли почуватися своїми.

Я пишу напіванонімно, як Ніхто, не тому, що хочу уникнути відповідальності за ці спостереження, а тому, що це не лише моя історія: вона належить колегам, друзям і подругам, яких я не називатиму, процесам, які можу описати лише узагальнено, проєкту, який я досі волію захищати, навіть коли беру під сумнів дещо із того, що відбулося в межах і навколо нього. Я пишу на запрошення долучитися до цієї книжки з перспективи когось, хто займає *проміжне* становище — достатньо включений, щоб побачити, але й достатньо виключений, щоб маркуватися як сторонній спостерігач. Це не претензія на об'єктивність; це конкретна точка зору з конкретними сліпими плямами та специфічними лініями видимості.

Я усвідомлюю, що описане нижче сформоване лише моїм досвідом, який є незначним порівняно із тим, що українці/-ки переживають щодня, — що б він не означав особисто для мене. Я намагався відокремити свої спостереження від своїх відчуттів, але мені це не зовсім вдалося. Тож я можу принаймні визнати цю невдачу й писати насамперед з позиції солідарності з українською боротьбою за виживання й суверенітет — не попри критику, що послідує нижче, а саме через неї.

Основа

Мені роками було важко зрозуміти, чому в деяких колег — людей, яких я вважав однодумцями/-ицями приблизно мого віку — це переконання з'явилося швидко, наче рефлекс: наполягання на тому, що я ніколи вповні не зрозумію Київ, що я не звідси, що моя присутність була одночасно необхідною (бо нам потрібні були «європейські стандарти», «міжнародні зв'язки», «першокласна експертиза») та нелегітимною (бо як сторонній сміє претендувати на формування чогось, що мало стати автентично українським). Звичайно, так вважали не всі — багато з них підходили до роботи по-іншому та не обов'язково розглядали співпрацю як запеклу боротьбу за автентичність. Проте алгоритм був достатньо послідовним і чітким, щоб зрештою структурувати те, як ухвалювалися рішення, що було прийнятно висловлювати, і хто міг говорити без попереднього зауваження: «Ну звісно, ти ж не звідси».

Мені потрібно було занадто багато часу, щоб зрозуміти, мабуть, очевидне: йшлося зовсім не про мене. Люди, які артикулювали це найчіткіше, не були зовнішніми критиками, а колегами на впливових

позиціях, які допомагали будувати те, що будували ми. Проте дещо таки залишалося непроясненим — наче проєкт міг бути повністю їхнім лише за умови, що він не був частково моїм. Можливо, вони мали рацію. Можливо, я дійсно репрезентував асиметрію ресурсів і впливовості, що відтворювали ті самі ієрархії, які ми намагалися руйнувати. Можливо, спрацьовували історичні контексти, які були мені недоступні, — я не міг знати напевно. Але позиціонування мене як стороннього надавало точку зору, з якої певні механізми ставали видимими: як працює питання приналежності, яку роль воно відіграє, хто може його ставити і хто мусить на нього відповідати. Я стояв на межі, де негласні правила зазвичай доводилося озвучувати, і часто вони працювали проти мене. Я не мав змоги контролювати, як зчитувалася моя присутність. Міг лише помічати, яким є це прочитання.

Утім, звести ці п'ять років до цієї єдиної динаміки означало б викреслити те, що насправді наповнювало цей проєкт, — тисячі людей, переважно українська (але не тільки) молодь, яка приходила кожних вихідних, годинами стояла в черзі взимку, приїжджала з інших міст. Вони миттєво й інстинктивно зрозуміли, чим бажало стати це місце. Це були люди, які чекали саме на це — секс-позитивний, дружній до квір-людей простір, де забороняється зйомка, а осуд залишається за дверима. Де можна танцювати, не хизуючись. Де все це могло просто проживатися, а не дискутуватися, реалізуючись через рухи тіл на танцполі та структури турботи, які ми побудували, щоб їх об'єднувати. У цих юрбах була відкритість, спрага до зв'язку поза кордонами — лінгвістичними, національними,

сексуальними, — відчувалася щира цікавість до відмінності, готовність до зустрічі з незнайомим. Можливо, це було пов'язано з тим, що простір ще був новим, здобутим зусиллями і поки не сприймався як належне. У Києві ця відкритість здавалася необхідною, обережною та живою — відчуття, які, сподіваюся, ніколи не будуть втрачені.

Клуб став одним із вузлів у мережі просторів-однодумців. Думаю, що саме це губиться у всіх дискусіях про автентичність та зовнішній вплив: те, що простір спрацював не тому, що він нав'язував щось зовні, а тому, що зрезонував із чимось уже присутнім усередині — бажанням, яке існувало в Києві задовго до нашого прибуття, жагою до саме такої свободи, відкритості, до саме такого світу. Ми не згенерували це бажання, а лише побудували для нього структуру. За п'ять років я мав десь тисячу розмов із тими, хто приходили, — на барі, в курилці, у черзі. Питання автентичності ніколи не поставало. Жодного разу. Вони просто присвоювали цей простір, реалізовували його через акт своєї присутності. Дискурс автентичності виник не там, а серед культурних журналістів/-ок та самопризначених арбітрів. І я почав замислюватися, яку функцію він насправді виконував.

Межа

Те, що спочатку було продуктивною напругою — побудовою чогось попри розбіжності, — згодом зайшло у глухий кут: чи був цей простір автентично українським, чи моя залученість свідчила про те, що таким він бути не міг? Я дедалі більше опинявся серед розмов, у яких припускалося, що це єдині можливі варіанти.

Пам'ятаю розмову на Трухановому острові з людиною, яку я поважав — відкритою та інтернаціонально орієнтованою, — у якій мені зі своєрідною обережною терплячістю пояснювали, що, *безумовно*, клуб важливий, безумовно, він є втіленням чогось істотного, проте невже я не бачу проблеми… оптики: того, що *іноземець* брав участь у створенні цього простору? Що це говорить про Україну, про українців і те, чи здатні ми формувати власну сучасність? Наче моя присутність свідчила, що не здатні.

Я швидко зрозумів, що мої запитання лише погіршували ситуацію, оскільки могли зчитуватися як захисна реакція, як небажання слухати. Але я хотів запитати: звідки саме прийшли такі цінності? Чому квірність вважалася чимось західним? Як щодо квір-людей Києва, які були там завжди? Чи жага до просторів без ієрархій була переважно імпортована? А як щодо людей, котрі до цього роками організовували андеграундні вечірки? Чи спрага до свободи була чимось, що ми привезли, чи радше розпізнали й, зрезонувавши з нею, побудували навколо неї структуру?

Я розумів біль у цьому твердженні, відчув у ньому історію, якої сам не пережив, і почав визнавати, що це не та напруга, яку можна зняти лише за допомогою часу або спільної роботи. Амбівалентність була від початку присутня. Новим було лише зростання моєї впевненості у тому, що вона ніколи не зникне. Проте мене не полишало питання, *чому*: з якою легкістю звучало слово «*іноземець*» навіть від тих колег, які відкидали грубші форми націоналізму. Вони вживали його суто дескриптивно, не помічаючи, що як означник воно виконувало певну функцію: поділу, категоризації, встановлення того, хто може

висловлюватися як інсайдер, а хто буде позначений зірочкою. Словник міг бути м'якшим, але я почав замислюватися, чи логіка, що була в його основі, була аж настільки відмінною, наскільки декому хотілось вірити.

Тіні

До 2021 року проблема того, хто був своїм стала відчуватися по-іншому — поступово, наче прихід зими у Київ. Щодо клубу завжди був спротив — передбачуваний гнів консерваторів через квірність і наркотики. Але тепер прийшло щось жорсткіше — організовані групи, що не послуговувалися дискурсом чи дискусіями, а приходили в балаклавах і з димовими шашками. Вони обґрунтовували своє насильство як захист «справжніх» українських цінностей проти західної дегенеративності, позиціонуючи квір-простори як нав'язані іноземцями, а квір-людей — як принципово не властивих українськості як такій. Пам'ятаю, як хтось вперше жбурнув пляшку у вхідні двері, як ми майже розсміялися, сприйнявши це як безглузде хуліганство, поки не розуміючи, що це була перевірка нашої захищеності, нашої реакції і того, чи хтось за нас заступиться. Поліція цього робити, звичайно, не збиралася — вони продемонстрували це через власні систематичні утиски: свавільні обшуки на наркотики, паркування своїх авто достатньо близько, щоб залякати, але достатньо далеко, щоб виправдати своє невтручання.

На кінець листопада 2021 року спроби зривів подій у вихідні стали майже рутиною — щосуботи протягом осені з'являлися ті самі групи, ті самі балаклави, ті самі поліціянти, які стояли поруч, курили,

спостерігали і обережно не втручалися, коли час від часу через стіни старої фабрики летіли каміння й запалені предмети. Річниця клубу відрізнялася хіба що своїм масштабом: міжнародні діджеї/-ки, понад тисяча людей, що чекають на морозі, а біля входу — близько тридцять замаскованих чоловіків блокують доступ і п'ятнадцять поліціянтів стоять неподалік. Протягом дев'яноста хвилин посередник вів переговори, а поліція наполягала, що ми порушуємо громадський спокій. Зрештою під тиском тисячі людей, що стояли на вулиці у морозну погоду, ворота відкрили. Та в моїй пам'яті закарбувався образ тих поліціянтів/-ок, що тижнями спостерігали, як молодим квір-людям погрожували, нічого не робили, наполягали, що проблема в нас, за замовчуванням погоджуючись із нападниками.

Пізніше ми переконалися у тому, що всі підозрювали: блокади оплачував конкурентний забудовник, і схоже, що у той час ці фінансові інтереси перетиналися з ідеологічними цілями ультраправих груп навколо Євгена Карася — фігури, чиї мережі були причетні до нападів на відкриті до квір-людей простори по всьому Києву. Після вторгнення інші розслідування вказали на дещо значно тривожніше: деякі ультраправі рухи, що діяли в Україні до 2022 року, могли бути інфільтровані чи опосередковано підтримувалися російськими агентами впливу. Однак у той момент я був уже просто виснажений. Здавалося, що ми вели боротьбу, яку вже програли — не тому, що опоненти були сильнішими, а тому, що вони ніколи не грали за жодними правилами.

Інверсія

24 лютого 2022 року. Повномасштабне вторгнення змінило все, проте варто трохи замислитися саме над тим, як воно змінило порядок того, кого можна було критикувати і які питання можна було ставити.

Чоловіки, чиєю мішенню ми були раніше — мережі навколо Карася, — тепер були на передовій. Багато з них воювали. Декотрі гинули. Що б не думали про їхню політику, своїми тілами вони стримували навалу на шляху до міста. Цей факт перевернув усі інші міркування, змусив усю попередню критику виглядати дріб'язковою — наче скарги людей, які мали розкіш перейматися гомофобією, коли на столицю насувалися танки. Я розумів це і відчував сам — запаморочення від того, що вдячність і критику стало неможливо висловлювати одночасно, а питання, які я ставив раніше, стали невимовними не тому, що вони отримали відповіді, а тому, що війна зробила їхню постановку схожою на зраду.

Утім, вторгнення не тільки реабілітувало тих, хто на нас нападав, але й підсвітило на те, що я помічав з 2018 року, — буденність, з якою багато молоді сприймали певні фашистські символи: «чорне сонце», витатуюване на чиїйсь гомілці, Вольфсанґель на шевроні. Культурні ґейткіпери, які так багато говорили про автентичність, помітно менше могли сказати про це. «Чорне сонце» створили окультисти Гайнріха Гіммлера, у нього немає іншої історії, та про це чомусь ніколи йшлося.

Тепер ті, хто носили ці символи, воювали на фронті, стаючи героями. Я бачив, як кампанії зі збору коштів на Заході не могли підтримувати певні підрозділи — батальйон «Азов», який захищав

Маріуполь у нещадних боях, став символом українського спротиву, але досі носив емблему із «чорним сонцем». Сформований німецьким контекстом, де ці символи однозначні й неприпустимі, я маю до них конкретне ставлення, яке не дозволяє не бачити певні речі, а інші, ймовірно, затьмарює. А втім, я так і не знайшов способу поставити ці питання публічно й не наражав себе на звинувачення в тому, що застосовую німецькі рамки в контексті, якого не розумію сповна. По суті, я сам брав участь у мовчанці, яку тут описую. Мені запам'яталась структура цієї мовчанки — не власне незгода чи інше тлумачення, яке я міг би запропонувати, а відчуття того, що сама постановка питання означала б, що я накладаю чужі рамки на контекст, де вони не працюють. І до, і під час вторгнення ця розбіжність залишалась незмінною. Мене турбує те, що нормалізується за такого мовчання, зокрема мого власного.

Стіни

До 2023 року дещо змінилося — не лише в тому, як трактували мою присутність, а й у тому, як саме питання приналежності дискутувалося в українському суспільстві. Нові розколи з'являлися навіть там, де війна вимагала солідарності. Я спостерігав за формуванням цих розривів у розмовах, у групових чатах, у коротких митях, коли комусь давали зрозуміти, що вони не зробили достатньо, не залишилися достатньо надовго, не пожертвували належним чином. Ті, хто залишилися, проти тих, хто поїхали. Ті, хто воювали, проти тих, хто ховалися від призову.

Розмежування спрямовувалися всередину (українці/-ки проти українців/-ок) й назовні проти будь-кого, хто вважався чужим. Пам'ятаю, як Макрон

зателефонував Путіну на початку вторгнення, і поширювався заклик «скасувати усіх французів/-ок» — наче всю країну можна звести до телефонного дзвінка її президента. Міжнародні колаборації тихо переривалися. Музикантів/-ок, які раніше регулярно грали, перестали запрошувати. Повідомлення колег залишалися непрочитаними, а їхню залученість переглядали як таку, що вже не потрібна.

Я став помічати певний впізнаваний патерн, хоча підозрюю, що він виходив за межі лише мого досвіду — своєрідна циклічність, коли умови для участі поступово усуваються, а потім твоя відсутність стає доказом недостатньої активності. Часткова відсутність стає доказом неповної відданості, виправдовуючи подальше дистанціювання і засвідчуючи початкову підозру. Чи це навмисно, чи просто так складаються обставини — можливо, це не має значення. Моє проміжне становище дозволило мені побачити цей патерн саме тому, що я став об’єктом переосмислення: я спостерігав, як роки співпраці переписувалися з надзвичайною швидкістю — не зовсім виклеслювалися, але відходили на другий план як менш важливі, ніж колись. Ті, хто здійснював переосмислення, можливо, сприймали це як закономірне уточнення, необхідне пристосування до нових реалій. З моєї точки зору це виглядало як механізм, що після запуску вже не зупиниться на таких, як я.

Мене хвилює те, що станеться, коли ця логіка вийде за межі надзвичайного стану — коли мережам, що з’єднували Україну зі світом, дозволять атрофуватися, а сама відкритість опиниться під підозрою. Відносини, на побудову яких пішли роки, можуть бути зруйновані за кілька місяців. Відновити їх буде важче.

Уламки

Яким би не був мій досвід поступового виключення, він був незначним порівняно з переживаннями інших. Розколи торкалися всіх по-різному. Жінка з Херсона, яка провела місяці за волонтерською роботою під час окупації — російськомовна, тому що це була мова її батьків, — повернулася до Києва і зіткнулася з підозрами, корекціями та прохолодою, яка промовляла: твоя російська є ознакою чогось не зовсім українського, хоча ти допомагала й ніколи не виїжджала. Становище тих, хто ніколи й не мали повного права на приналежність — квір-людей, меншин, тих, хто не вписувалися в новий національний наратив, — стало ще більш непевним.

Від початку вторгнення квір-українці/-ки організовувались так, що їхня приналежність здавалась незаперечною: формували власні військові підрозділи, засновували ГО для підтримки військових-ЛГБТ+ на фронті, водночас виживали й чинили спротив. Багато з них робили все, що начебто мало значення: воювали, волонтерили, організовували взаємопідтримку. А втім, залишалися вони чи виїжджали, їхнє становище ставало дедалі безвихіднішим: залишитися й опинитися в майбутньому, де чоловіки, що полювали на тебе до війни, повернулися озброєними недоторканими героями; поїхати і втратити все — друзів, право на повернення і приналежність, яка наполегливо виборювалася роками.

Друг, який був частиною спільноти від початку — відкритий квір, який роками боровся за своє право на існування в Києві, — після вторгнення працював із військовими підрозділами, борючись із дискримінацією зсередини. Він роками не виїжджав, наполягаючи на своїй приналежності, аж поки не

вирішив, що більше не може. Він утік через зелений кордон до ЄС, ризикуючи затриманням, ризикуючи всім. Наслідки були миттєві: друзі перервали зв'язок, і тепер він не може повернутися додому хтозна-скільки років, поки їздить з країни в країну по всій Європі. «Я роками доводив, що моє місце там, — сказав він мені. — У певний момент я усвідомив, що не повинен нічого доводити».

Улітку 2025 року хтось, пов'язаний з мережами Карася — тими ж групами, що нападали на нас 2021 року, — прийшов до клубу зі зброєю, погрожував охороні й вимагав, щоб його пропусили всередину. Про інцидент так і не заявили. Не тому, що він був несерйозний, а тому, що заявити означало би звинуватити когось, хто воював на передовій, і в теперішній атмосфері це виглядало б як зрада самого війська. Саме це турбує мене найбільше: не те, що насильство відбувається, а те, що про певне насильство неможливо повідомити. Групи, що нападали на квір-простори, тепер офіційно озброєні та володіють статусом участі в бойових діях. Питання не в тому, чи скористаються вони цією владою, — вони вже це роблять. Питання в тому, що стається, коли певні люди стають недоторканими, а статус захисника отримують ті, чиї мішені не змінилися.

Горизонти

Треті простори не є вторинними й не є додатками, які постають після того, як «справжню роботу» зроблено. Це місця, де суспільство, за яке борються, формується в мініатюрі. Тисячі людей, що приходять до клубу кожних вихідних, не втікають від реальності — вони її створюють. І той факт, що це відбувається вночі, з музикою і танцями, не робить це менш

значущим, ніж щоденна робота над законодавством і політичним курсом. Можливо, це щось навіть більш основоположне, тому що саме так люди інтуїтивно й колективно відчувають, як це — жити в суспільстві, організованому за принципами, відмінними від домінування і контролю. Коли ви це відчули, ви не зможете цього забути.

Однак ці свободи не гарантовані. Питання того, як поводитися з групами, символами та ідеологіями, які допомогли врятувати країну, але загрожують свободам, за які ця країна нібито бореться, не можна уникати вічно, не можна відкладати до якогось уявного післявоєнного моменту, коли нюанси стануть прийнятними. Це відбувається зараз, у тому, як ми говоримо про тих, хто воював, і про те, за що вони воювали, у тому, як певні символи нормалізуються, а певна критика витісняється.

І ось що часто губиться у дискурсі виживання: Україна бореться за щось, а не лише проти чогось. За свободу — існування без страху, без необхідності обґрунтовувати свою присутність. За демократію — суспільство, де можна висловлювати незгоду без навішування ярликів про зраду. За самовизначення — право на участь кожної людини у формулюванні того, що означає «ми». Такі принципи неможливо захищати в теорії і водночас порушувати їх на практиці. Саме у третіх просторах вони реалізуються.

Формування цього майбутнього вимагатиме участі всіх українців/-ок — тих, хто залишилися і тих, хто виїхали, тих, хто воювали і тих, хто зробили свій внесок у інший спосіб, тих, хто вписується у нові наративи і тих, хто ніколи не вписувалися. Це вимагатиме переосмислення співпраці як сили, а критики — як турботи. І ще дечого важчого — готовності миритися

з дискомфортом, опиратися бажанню зняти кожну напругу, визначаючи, хто належить до спільноти, а хто — ні. Треті простори довели, що це здійсненно: що сила полягає у відкритості, що суспільство може непохитно захищати свій суверенітет, водночас залишаючись щиро відкритим до відмінностей.

Ця здатність — відкритість, яку я бачив її у тих юрбах, щира цікавість до відмінностей — досі існує, хоч і пошкоджена, проте функціональна. Чи переживе вона майбутні виклики, залежатиме від українців/-ок та тисячі малих рішень щодо того, чиї голоси мають значення, які простори заслуговують на захист, заради якого суспільства все це було. Майбутнє України визначатимуть не ті, хто претендує на найбільш автентичний зв'язок з її минулим, а ті, хто візьметься за будівництво цього майбутнього. Я можу лише сказати, що це було можливим. І сподіваюся, що це чогось варте, навіть приїзду когось, хто зрештою виявився ніким ●

Ніхто прибув до Києва у 2018 році, щоб працювати над простором, якого не існує.

Мерехтіння

Мені здається, так могло би виглядати пекло —
Блискуча споруда зі скла і металу: кілька рівнів угору,
    кілька кілець униз.
Усі поспішають і нудяться у напруженому чеканні.
Еврідіка дочекалася свого потяга, Персефона
    підіймається на ескалаторі,
Харон у водонепроникному комбінезоні гортає своє
    весло далі.
А головне — усіх забагато — це повня, надлишок,
    гамір.
Акція на крильця жар-птиці. Вогонь тане на язиці.
Вириваюся з цього виру, біжу у прохолоду ночі,
    до озера, цілую стіну будинку над ним.
Хто сказав, що справжнє завжди блискавичне?
    Гроза?
Повільно йду каналом вулиці — Небо сьогодні таке
    зіркове!
«На східному фронті дають
найвидовищнішу з вистав».
Десь на півночі у пилку своїх коридорів задихається
    сірий песиголовець.
Он зірка вказує йому шлях у Тартарію.
Повільно-повільно випливає човник місяця,
щоб перевезти його у... але ні, і цього не вийде —
дірявий, прострілений осколком моєї країни.
Мерехтить моральний закон в середині нас.

Юлія Стахівсьна, 2023

Про кров і найрадикальніший жест турботи.

Нотатки про мистецтво під час війни

Оксана Брюховецька

«Коли на тілі є відкрита рана — вона спочатку кровоточить або гниє. Її лікують, і вона поступово загоюється, вкриваючись шкірочкою з крові, що запеклася», — ці слова написала до свого проєкту українська художниця Юлія Данилевська, яка на початку повномасштабного російського вторгнення в Україну деякий час прожила в окупованому Херсоні. Робота Юлії базується на інтерв'ю з нейровідмінними художницями, зробленими 2025 року, і має назву «Рана скресла як крига». Вона розмовляла з мистикнями про те, як нейровідмінність впливає на їхні практики — не тільки на творчість, але й на співпрацю з інституціями, здатність відповідати вимогам мистецького світу. Цей проєкт Юлія здійснила, за її словами, намагаючись подолати власну психологічну кризу. Жест художниці полягає ось у чому: якщо тобі важко — ти звертаєшся до тих, хто страждає також і кому, можливо, ще важче. Цей жест виходить за межі мистецтва, він радше працює як жест турботи, спонукою до якої є власне страждання. Ці розмови проявили те, що бар'єри створює не лише нейровідмінний стан. Бар'єри часто створені застановами, на яких побудований мистецький світ, такими як конкурентність, ієрархічність, фокус на продуктивності й успіхові. У моїй передмові до книжки[1], де опублікований проєкт, я написала:

Це маленьке дослідження Юлії має значення у набагато ширшому контексті. Ментальні особливості — не лише вроджені та сталі. Психологічні проблеми і психічні розлади виникають на будь-якому етапі життя, спричинені зовнішніми стресовими чинниками. В Україні, де вже 11 років війна, величезна кількість людей потребують

підтримки і допомоги. Нам потрібно облаштовувати суспільне життя на абсолютно інших засадах — не на тих, де пробивається сильніший, а на тих, де ми піклуємося одне про одного, підтримуємо тих, кому важко.

Коли я кажу про те, що проєкт виходить за межі мистецтва, це значить, що він стає суспільною практикою турботи. Втім, згодом він повертається в мистецтво у формі мистецької роботи чи тексту. Шкірочка з крові, що запеклася, яка захищає рану і забезпечує їй можливість зцілення — це метафора того, як може працювати мистецтво, коли є потреба подолати власну психологічну кризу. Такі практики нині існують в українському суспільстві і мистецтві часто поза інституціями і фінансуванням. Вони зближуються з практиками волонтерства і зборів донатів для українських військових, які поширилися у час повномасштабної війни.

Міркуючи про турботу і вихід за межі мистецтва, я стикаюся з питанням: чи не є рішення піти на фронт воювати — що в нашому випадку означає захищати — найрадикальнішим жестом суспільної турботи у наш спотворений війною час? Деякі художники і художниці здійснили цей найрадикальніший із жестів — пішли воювати за Україну. Деякі з тих, хто пішли, загинули. Загибель митців і мисткинь — як от квір-художника і музиканта Артура Сніткуса 2024 року, Маргарити Половінко і Давида Чичкана 2025 року — стають травматичними подіями, які згуртовують мистецьку спільноту в актах скорботи. Ці смерті також є розривами в мистецькій бульбашці, які зв'язують її з набагато ширшою спільнотою людей, які пішли на фронт і загинули.

Кажуть, що художник Давид Чичкан, ідучи на війну, казав: «Я нічим не кращий від тих інших, хто воюють на фронті», що буквально означало — «їм зараз найважче, і я піду туди».

Коли тіло художника й анархіста Давида Чичкана лежало у відкритій труні на Майдані Незалежності — місці українських революцій, — довкола була маса людей і прапорів: анархістських, феміністських, ЛГБТК, українських. Поруч із труною стояли в ряд роздруковані роботи — малюнки Давида. Згодом ця виставка перемістилася на цвинтар, де відбулося останнє прощання і поховання в оточенні численної публіки, друзів і рідних. Незадовго до того, як Давид пішов на війну, його нову виставку скасував Одеський художній національний музей через погрози ультраправих опонентів художника: на його роботах були представлені анархісти й так звані «неавторитарні ліві», товариші і товаришки, які воюють за Україну чи загинули за неї. Це був проєкт про різноманіття політичних поглядів в українській армії, про те, що захисники та захисниці України відчувають відповідальність за те, якою вони хочуть її бачити. На одній зі своїх робіт Давид змалював образ України, за яку віддав життя: «Незалежна, самостійна, антиавторитарна, безкласова, прогресивна, феміністична, соціальна, соціалістична». Ця візія майбутнього, описана Давидом у його радикально-утопічній манері, назавжди буде переплетена з пам'яттю про нього. Майбутнє, яке відбудовуватимуть ті, хто залишаться і хто знали Давида, буде освітлене нею. Ця думка, спрямована в майбутнє, насправді черпає натхнення з минулого: на малюнку, який прикрашає цей напис, зображені увічнені українські

мислителі минулого — Михайло Драгоманов, Леся Українка та Іван Франко[2].

Майдан зібрав усю мистецьку спільноту, яка тільки була в той день у Києві, і не лише її. Біля труни стояла Ганна Циба, дружина Давида і моя подруга, а поруч у дитячому візочку спав їхній восьмимісячний син Нестор. Я бачила дорослих чоловіків, які ридали. Сама ж натомість відчувала якесь оніміння, все було залите болем, увесь навколишній міський пейзаж, але я немов не відчувала цього болю, як під час ковіду дехто не відчували смаку. Я навіть питала себе — де він, той біль? У дні після того, як дізналась про загибель Давида, я іноді спонтанно починала плакати — рана наче відкривалася час од часу, біль надходив приступами, це було часто. Думаю, для багатьох очевидно: Давид залишається з нами у нашій пам'яті, а також у його малюнках. З дня смерті художника чи художниці ми завжди дивимося на їхні роботи трохи інакше. Дивовижним чином їхні роботи полегшують біль від втрати — вони немов та шкірочка із запеченої крові, яка захищає рану, завдану їхньою смертю.

Всередині ми наповнені кров'ю — це значить, ми наповнені життям. Втрата крові, рана, що кровоточить, є ознакою, що смерть підступила близько. На роботі, намальованій художницею Маргаритою Половінко власною кров'ю, смерть по-буденному близько перебуває поруч біля чоловіка. Маргарита, яка пішла воювати на фронт, залишила собі два медіуми для своїх малюнків — простий олівець, яким малювала янголів, що кричать у відповідь на кожну вбиту росіянами дитину, і власну кров. Після загибелі Маргарити влітку 2025 року її малюнки, зроблені кров'ю, змінюють колір — на тих, що опубліковані

онлайн іще за життя, колір крові яскравіший. На фото з оригіналів, які зроблені після її загибелі, їхній колір темно-бурий: кров, відділена від тіла, з часом змінює відтінок — вона існує незалежно від нього.

Кров як мистецький медіум підводить до осмислення формули, яка є щоденною і буденною у час війни: ти або ще живеш, або вже мертвий. Ця формула виводить з фокусу зору всю складність і розмаїття життєвого досвіду, спрощуючи його до однієї константи: «ти все ще живеш». Нічого, окрім цього, більше не має значення з того, що залишилось на боці життя. У такий спосіб смерть захоплює територію життя у час, коли життя ще триває. Вона наче відбирає відчуття смаку, відчуття болю. Так само вночі під час обстрілів розпорошується мій страх — він наче десь навколо мене, всюди, але я вже не усвідомлюю, мені страшно чи ні — відчуваю лише напругу в усьому тілі. Після ночі обстрілів, гортаючи новини про руйнування і смерті у місті, я наче вже й не вражена й не здивована, я відчуваю той самий заморожений стан, як на прощанні з Давидом.

Та немає більшої втіхи зранку після безсонної ночі обстрілів, як вийти на вулицю Києва і побачити людей, які спрямовано кудись простують, а інші вигулюють собак, а ще інші — п'ють каву на лавочках чи в кафе. На вулиці — життя, і страх вивітрюється з квартири після того, як відкрити штори і вікна. Маленькі буденні дії і речі оживають, незважаючи на те, що російські ракети всю ніч летіли на нас і несли в собі смерть. Маленькі буденні дії і речі також покривають рану тривожної ночі шкіркою.

Мистецтво теж тепер часто звертається до буденних речей. Київські кураторка і психологиня Дана Брежнєва і фотомисткиня Наталка Дяченко разом

здійснюють тривалий мистецький проєкт «Ательє чудес Дани і Наталки», винесений за межі мистецтва у буденне життя жінок. Вони розпочали проект 2023 року на Закарпатті, працюючи з переміщеними особами. Відвідавши Ательє, жінки отримують доглядові процедури за обличчям і макіяж, а потім фотосесію. Під час цього процесу точаться розмови про життя, досвід війни і стрес та про можливість дбати про себе серед усього цього. Навесні 2025 року Ательє мандрувало прифронтовими територіями на Сході України. Дана і Наталка працювали в містах Донеччини — Краматорську, Слов'янську, Святогірську. Жінки і дівчата-підлітки, мешканки частково розбомблених прифронтових міст, отримували сесії турботи, а їхні фотопортрети згодом ставали частиною їхнього домашнього архіву і частиною портфоліо художниць. Дана і Наталка пишуть в своєму репортажі про поїздку: «Це не про зовнішність — це про те, як ми можемо повертати собі себе через тілесність, образ, дотик до краси». Даруючи моменти радості іншим, Дана і Наталка отримують їх взамін і для себе: «Для нас Фотоательє — кажуть вони, — це також своєрідна реабілітація та спосіб зосередитися на цінних повсякденних моментах»[3].

У лютому 2025 року я потрапляю в гості до кураторки Олександри Погребняк на квартирну виставку у її приватному помешканні на лівому березі Дніпра у Києві. Квартирні виставки поширилися останнім часом, іноді це разові акції у когось вдома, іноді — постійна діяльність, як на квартирі у художниці Тамари Турлюн або у «Балконній галереї» на Подолі, організованій кураторкою Оксаною Озарчук.

Саша Погребняк має дворічного сина Тео, а її чоловік недавно мобілізувався[4]. Так збіглося, що

Сашин день народження припадає на 24 лютого, день, коли Росія розпочала проти нас повномасштабну війну. Вона вирішує замість щорічно святкувати день народження (як тепер «святкувати», якщо це початок війни?) щорічно цього дня проводити вдома виставку, присвячену річниці початку війни, і запрошувати додому людей на цю публічну подію. Мистецтво стає захисною шкіркою для рани, якої зазнало найінтимніше свято.

Зайшовши в квартиру — мене туди привела художниця і кураторка Марина Мариніченко, — ми бачимо роботи на стінах у великій залі і людей, які скупчилися при вході у ванну кімнату. Я зазираю крізь плечі й голови і бачу зі спини художницю Катю Лібкінд, яка за маленьким столиком у ванній кімнаті перебирає на своєму ноутбуці власний цифровий архів (диджитальний компост, як вона описала його згодом у приватній розмові). Катя Лібкінд разом з іншою художницею, Катею Бучацькою, вже кілька років працює з нейровідмінними людьми і планує відкрити мистецький простір для їхніх мистецьких практик.

Я помічаю на підлозі пляму крові. Оскільки стоїть тиша і ніхто нічого не пояснює, я тільки згодом дізнаюсь від одного з гостей про те, що відбувається. Проникнувши глибше всередину ванної кімнати, бачу дійство на власні очі: у той час як Катя гортає вкладки на ноутбуці, до її руки приєднаний катетер. Він з'єднаний трубкою із прозорим медичним мішком, наповненим кров'ю, який висить закріплений на стіні. Як мені пояснили, кров була відібрана з однієї руки, а тепер переливається назад у тіло, в іншу руку. Дійство нагадує медичну процедуру, акт саморуйнування або самопожертви. Спочатку мені

геть незрозуміло, навіщо художниця робить це зі своїм тілом заради мистецтва — адже в анонсі події це оголошено перформансом. Назва перформансу — «Янгол, що згортає небо».[5]

Відбір крові у мішок і повернення її назад у тіло (кількість відібраної крові сягала 450 мл) тривало близько 30 хвилин. Опісля глядачі й художниця покинули ванну кімнату і розмістилися у великій залі, де Саша, кураторка, зустріла гостей вітальним словом. Я підсіла на підлогу поруч із Катею, щоб запитати в неї, що її перформанс для неї означає. Хоча в мене були власні інтерпретації, замішані на почуттях піднесеності, страху і відрази, мені завжди цікаво слухати, що художниця чи художник самі кажуть про свою роботу. Катя відповіла коротко і просто, що в роботі насправді немає особливого змісту, окрім буквальної ідеї виходу з власного тіла і повернення в тіло назад. В дійсності ця акція є вправою, яку Катя навчилася робити на курсах бойових медиків «Госпітальєрів[6]». Трансфузію — переливання крові — яке можливо треба буде зробити іншій людині, тренуються робити, як я з'ясувала, на собі. Це просте і прозаїчне пояснення знизило градус страху, з яким я початково сприйняла роботу, і показало її як цитування практик і навичок турботи, вкорінених у часі воєнного стану. Художниця під примусом війни здобуває кваліфікацію медсестри — вона виходить за межі мистецької діяльності. Але Катя ділиться досвідом, що як художниця, опановуючи цю вправу, вона побачила в ній чистий, самодостатній і завершений мистецький жест. Перформанс і є цим жестом: ця робота, за словами художниці — чиста форма.

Квартирна виставка до річниці початку війни, вправа з переливання крові як мистецький

 Про кров і найрадикальніший жест турботи

перформанс — це мистецькі дії у відповідь на війну. Мистецтво тут практикує вихід з тіла і повернення у нього, а також повернення собі власного дня народження у теплому колі спільноти, втім, із додатковим значенням, яке тепер несе цей день. Саша Погребняк так коментує свій виставковий проєкт:

У цій новій реальності я розглядаю ці квартирні виставки як феміністичну форму повернення собі приватного простору — не як відсторонення, а як позначення місця, де турбота, рефлексія та художня думка можуть співіснувати, пропонуючи індивідуалізовану форму опору та спосіб залишатися присутніми посеред постійного розриву.[7]

У помешканні Саші Погребняк я знаходжу на полиці серед книжок каталог виставки «Українське тіло», яку я курувала в 2012 році разом з Лесею Кульчинською у Центрі візуальної культури, що в той час знаходився в Києво-Могилянській академії. Цю виставку тоді цензурував президент академії Сергій Квіт, зачинивши її на ключ через окремі роботи на теми сексуальності та тілесності. Я дістаю каталог, щоб показати присутнім роботу Олександра Володарського з назвою «Зелена пляшка, наповнена червоною рідиною» (2012), яку від зробив тоді для виставки. Це була пляшка, наповнена його власною кров'ю, яка стояла на полиці, і відеодокументація того, як він відбирав у себе кров. Робота присвячувалася політичним ув'язненим. Олександр став таким ув'язненим у 2011 році, після того, як його заарештували біля Верховної Ради під час оголеного перформансу: вони з подругою імітували біля державної установи

статевий акт. Перформанс був акцією протесту проти дій Національної експертної комісії із захисту моралі часів президентства Віктора Януковича, яка цензурувала фільми і книжки з темами тілесності, сексуальності та ЛГБТК. Через кілька днів після того, як виставку «Українське тіло» закрили, ми з Лесею Кульчинською зайшли у приміщення і побачили, що пляшка валяється поруч з бурою плямою крові на підлозі з дерев'яних дощок. Ми не дізналися, як це трапилося, втім, нас вразив цей збіг значень — на виставці буквально і метафорично пролилась кров, немов у відповідь на акт обмеження свободи висловлювання.

Поки ми гортали каталог, сидячи на підлозі у Сашиній квартирі, місточок був перекинутий між однією роботою про кров та іншою, тринадцяти-річної давності. Ці роботи належать різному часові, проте нашій єдиній українській історії мистецтва і також історії різних форм спротиву і боротьби за нашу свободу. Війна відрізає минуле, іноді важко зв'язати вчорашній день із сьогоднішнім, а тим паче попереднє десятиліття з нинішнім. Втім, нещо-давно дослідниці мистецтва Мілена Хомченко і Таня Жмурко запропонували мені написати текст про мої кураторські роботи у період між двома рево-люціями, протягом десятиліття між 2004 і 2014 роками. Дівчата працюють над книжкою, присвяче-ною мистецтву цього періоду. Я пишу текст для них і одночасно пишу цей текст. Це, власне, ще одна справа, якою ми займаємося в Україні під час війни: описуємо нашу турбулентну історію мистецтва для наступних поколінь.

Я не хочу дозволити війні накинути на мене свою тінь і заморозити мою пам'ять або переформатувати

моє сприйняття таким чином, щоб самоцензурувати себе чи приховувати якісь речі, які сьогодні можуть здаватися «неважливими». І це складно. Бо зі смертю, яка поруч, стосунки подвійні: те, чого вона хоче (а за її спиною російський агресор), — це позбавити і дрібних, і значних речей їхнього значення. Бо її формула проста: ти або ще живеш, або вже мертвий — максимально скорочена формула життя, що виводить з фокусу зору всю складність і розмаїття життєвого досвіду. Але те, що ми протиставляємо їй — і в цьому полягає другий аспект стосунків з нею (мистецтво не здаватися), — це надання значення значним речам і дрібним речам, буденним речам і фантазіям, історії країни та історії її мистецтва.

Життя проявляється, коли щось набуває значення. Все, чим наповнене життя, може давати сили для того, щоб жити. Життя — в новому макіяжі, який подарували Дана і Наталка жителькам поруйнованого російськими обстрілами міста. Життя у тому, щоб запросити додому друзів — на виставку і водночас на день народження. Життя у тому, щоб дбати про дитину, як Ганна дбає про Нестора, батько якого загинув на війні. Її щоденна турбота завжди існуватиме в світлі найрадикальнішого жесту, який здійснили Давид, Маргарита й інші митці, що доєдналися до багатьох інших, часом далеких від мистецтва захисників і захисниць на лінії фронту. Багато хто з них ніколи не повернеться. Своєю турботою вони врятували життя іншим.

Усе, чим наповнене життя, може давати сили для того, щоб жити. В цьому сила самовідновлення, як у випадку з кров'ю, яка виходить з тіла і повертається назад. Вийти за межі і повернутися назад —

це формула, підказана тренуванням із переливання крові задля порятунку життя. Найголовніше ж повернення, на яке ми всі сподіваємось, — це повернення до мирного життя, коли тиран, агресор і ворог буде переможений.

Кров здатна запікатися, перетворюючись на захисний шар для рани, — це одна з властивостей виживання людського тіла. Жести виходу за межі мистецтва згодом повертають мистецтву щось, а саме — властивість ставати захисною шкіркою, яка закриває рану. Мистецтво в Україні сьогодні слугує такою шкіркою для ментальних ран, завданих війною.

Жовтень 2025 ●

Оксана Брюховецька — художниця, кураторка, дослідниця та письменниця з Києва, Україна. Вона є редакторкою збірки проєктів українських художниць *Meaning after Loss* (2025) та авторкою книги *Black Lives Matter Voices* (Choven, 2025).

1   Art Stitches Ruptured Time Back Together. Introduction in the *Meaning After Loss*, edited by Oksana Briukhovetska. Martin Roth Initiative, 2025. Online access:https: //www.martin-roth-initiative.de/en/ukrainian-women-artists-publication.

2   Михайло Драгоманов, Леся Українка й Іван Франко — канонічні постаті української літератури і філософської думки кінця 19 — початку 20 століть, які мали національно-демократичні і соціалістичні погляди. Леся Українка, окрім іншого, визнана феміністкою того часу.

3   «Вірогідність того, що я загину — 0,01%»: пригоди «Фотоательє Чудес» на Донеччині. https://artslooker.com/virohidnist-toho-shcho-ia-zahynu-0-01-pryhody-fotoatelie-chudes-na-donechchyni/.

4   Чоловік Саші Погребняк, Дмитро Чепурний, також у цивільному житті є куратором.

5   Перформанс був багатошаровий — одночасно у пральній машині поруч прались шматки полотна з намальованими художницею етюдами неба, а у посудинні-ванні у піні плавали тілесні залишки іншого перформансу, що був представлений у виставці на відео, — глітер, лобкове волосся і білі накладні вії.

6   «Госпітальєри» — український волонтерський медичний батальйон, що бере участь у російсько-українській війні на Донбасі з 2014 року. Займається наданням першої медичної, домедичної допомоги та евакуацією поранених українських воїнів з найгарячіших ділянок фронту. (https://uk.wikipedia.org/wiki/)

7   Oleksandra Pogrebnyak. On Peace and Joy from an Apartment Exhibition in Kyiv. https://mostmagazine.org/2025/10/13/on-peace-and-joy-from-an-apartment-exhibition-in-kyiv/.

Привиди

Пейзаж усе той, але підмальовок холоду ледь синіє.
У ранкових туманах все більше виклику.
Злітають сталеві яструби — їх не видно — цих
    винищувачів,
але вони є за хмарами. Привиди.
А внизу таке саме погідне небо — альпійські луки з
    баранцями хмар —
збиває вітер у піну отару,
холодний вівчар.
Ні, не те, щоб нам страшно було,
не зовсім.
Зеленіє оком куплений кимось кавун на чиємусь
    вікні.
Твоя мама грає Баха.
Невтомний церковник...
Тільки вночі хтось виїдає серце маленькою
    ложечкою
і дзенькає нею по дну.

Юлія Стахівсьна, 2015

Гаражний кооператив

Аріна Янович

Між руїнами та стійністю

Існує водночас жорстока й заспокійлива істина: життя триває навіть під час війни. За виттям сирен, нескінченним потоком новин і повідомлень про втрати залишається людська потреба в сенсі, красі та скороминущому відчутті нормальності. Життя проростає крізь дим, відмовляючись згаснути.

Навіть руїни свідчать про цю наполегливість. Це не лише залишки минулого, а й зародки майбутнього — пороги ще не втіленого. Кожен колапс містить у собі контури відновлення. Відбудувати місто означає не просто відновити його стіни; це означає свідомо обрати, що суспільство збереже в пам'яті, а що вирішить втратити.

Та як міський розвиток, спрямований на колективне благо, може вкорінитися в суспільстві, де виживання — не метафора, а щоденна реальність?

Із кінця 1980-х років міста в усьому світі розвивалися за простою формулою: більше землі — більше прибутку. В Україні, зокрема в Києві, ця логіка перетворилася на майже безальтернативну доктрину у 1990-х і досі визначає будівельну політику — навіть в умовах війни. Однак межі цієї системи дедалі помітніші. Існують місця, про які міське планування воліє не згадувати: ділянки, що чинять опір комодифікації, де непомітно триває інший тип міського життя. На противагу відполірованим фасадам і спекулятивним хмарочосам, ці проміжні зони вперто зберігають людський вимір. Це не руїни минулого, а простори прояву альтернативної міської логіки — фрагменти міста, де зв'язок важливіший за капітал.

20 м² свободи

Як і в багатьох радянських історіях, усе почалося з дефіциту. У 1950-х роках приватний автомобіль став символом суспільного прогресу — особистою перемогою в межах колективного проєкту. Держава заохочувала володіння автомобілем як ознаку модерності та соціальної стабільності, однак не забезпечувала належної інфраструктури для паркування.

У відповідь на цю нестачу виникли гаражні кооперативи — напівофіційні форми самоорганізації, в межах яких люди власними зусиллями облаштовували індивідуальні гаражні простори, зазвичай на міських периферіях. Членство в кооперативі було бажаним, але вимагало терпіння, неформальних зв'язків і тривалої бюрократичної процедури: численних заяв, статутів, внесків і дозволів. Формально використання гаража суворо обмежувалося однією функцією — зберіганням автомобіля.

Неофіційно ж, як це часто траплялося в авторитарних системах, справжнє життя починалося там, де послаблювався контроль. За металевими дверима розгорталося паралельне існування: майстерні, сховки, клуби, простори усамітнення й камерних зустрічей. Те, що створювалося як утилітарна інфраструктура, поступово перетворилося на соціальний організм. Кожен гараж наповнювався інструментами, меблями, світлинами, колекціями та малими особистими історіями. У тісних рядах формувалися власні порядки й ритуали. Серед монотонних радянських житлових масивів виникало те, чого офіційно майже не передбачали: простір для індивідуальності — і водночас форма тихого спротиву, колективного життя в тіні режиму.

Гаражна країна

Гаражний кооператив «Киянівський» розташований на одному з найвиразніших пагорбів Києва — між Воздвиженкою та Пейзажною алеєю, в історичному районі, що зазнав інтенсивних трансформацій, комерційного «осучаснення» та приватизації. Дорога до нього проходить між вилощеними фасадами й занедбаними, зарослими ділянками. Поміж нових елітних будинків, руїн старих вілл і диких чагарників постає компактна, майже автономна територія. На вершині розкинулося плато з першим рядом гаражів. Деякі з них — двоповерхові — притулилися до схилу пагорба. Їхні стійкі бруталістські каркаси пом'якшують мох і виноградна лоза; радянський бетон переплітається з десятиліттями імпровізації.

Денні був одним із перших, хто побачив тут не занепад, а потенціал. Його діяльність не має формального статусу й полягає в уважному, поступовому переосмисленні вже наявних структур за допомогою мінімальних засобів. На початку 2025 року Денні разом із однодумцями почав орендувати окремі гаражі, очищати їх і тимчасово облаштовувати. Деякі приміщення досі зберігають матеріальні сліди минулого: фотопапір 1990-х років, непроявлені плівки, інструменти, радянську цеглу.

Подібно до 1980-х, гаражі знову стають просторами зустрічей — динамічними, самоорганізованими, живими. Тут відбуваються музичні події, кінопокази, виставки, чаювання, блошині ринки, ремонтні майстерні та нічні розмови, що тривають до світанку. Проєкт Денні об'єднує сусідів, митців і друзів у неформальну, але згуртовану спільноту. Особливо помітна участь молодих людей, які в умовах війни шукають нові форми спільного буття. У

жодному іншому контексті згуртованість цього покоління не проявляється так яскраво, як у цих імпровізованих просторах — острівцях соціальної близькості й довіри в розірваному війною повсякденні.

Одного разу Денні показав старий архітектурний план кооперативу: сітку симетрично розташованих прямокутних будівель без виразної ієрархії. План виглядає технічним і продуманим: кожен гараж пронумерований, на мапі збережені назви вулиць, зокрема Киянівський провулок, який існує й сьогодні. У центрі — трохи більша будівля, позначена як «охоронна споруда». Принцип невеликого поселення з комунальним центром відчувається тут і нині.

Місця, де дика природа переплітається зі старими, але життєздатними спорудами, стають дедалі рідкіснішими. Киянівський кооператив залишається винятковим палімпсестом: радянські фундаменти, археологічні нашарування та сучасні графіті. На вигляд хаотичний, але точний у своїй багатошаровості, він функціонує як живий архів міської пам'яті.

Втім, ця крихка екологія перебуває під загрозою. Стандартизована політика «благоустрою» може зруйнувати автентичність таких місць: асфальтовані доріжки, декоративні клумби, надмірне освітлення. Подібні шаблонні рішення ігнорують локальні практики та соціальний контекст. Натомість спільнота Денні пропонує простіший, але змістовніший підхід: зберегти територію у форматі громадського міського саду — простору співжиття природи й культури. Йдеться про озеленення, створення майданчиків для громадської активності, висадження дерев, що приваблюють міських птахів і підтримують локальне біорізноманіття.

Практика Денні формує естетику необхідного, повертаючи до первісної ідеї гаражних кооперативів — спільних дій у межах обмежених ресурсів. «Киянівський» є показовим прикладом таких ініціатив у Києві, що виникають у відповідь на дефіцит публічної інфраструктури та недовіру до часто корумпованого державного планування.

(сюр)реальна нерухомість

Із плато гаражного кооперативу відкривається вид на новозбудовані житлові комплекси. Квартал Воздвиженка є одним із найяскравіших прикладів провальної урбаністичної політики: еклектичне поєднання архітектурних стилів і символічних кодів без цілісної концепції. Пастельні орнаментовані фасади, різноманітні форми дахів, французькі балкони та постмодерні елементи вражають відсутністю масштабу й зв'язку з довкіллям. Те, що тут називають «старим містом», насправді є сконструйованою симуляцією — архітектурою, відірваною від історичної пам'яті та соціального життя. На цьому тлі гаражі вирізняються впертою автентичністю.

Поки інвестиційні проєкти орієнтуються на репрезентацію й прибуток, гаражний кооператив функціонує за логікою необхідності, де культура формується органічно[1]. Цей простір відмовляється від логіки симулякру[2], описаної Жаном Бодріяром: без інсценування та імітації — він відкритий, гнучкий і справжній. Культура тут не проєктується заздалегідь, а постає з повсякденного життя, випадкових зустрічей і спільних дій.

Культурна енергія народжується не в нейтральних, стандартизованих приміщеннях, а в зіткненнях, імпровізації та непередбачуваності.

Місто формується не лише через плани й проєкти, а насамперед через способи щоденного користування простором. Як довго такі місця зможуть існувати, перш ніж їх поглине комерційна логіка прибутку, — невідомо. Та саме в їхній тимчасовості полягає сила: вони плинні, відкриті й водночас стійкі. З їхнім зникненням ми втрачаємо більше, ніж їх фізичну присутність — зникає можливість розвитку поза заданими нормами, у просторах, де культура не інсценується, а проживається.

Можливо, Денні — реальний чи символічний, — це радше не постать, а принцип: виборювання автономії, дії та присутності. Разом із ним постає фундаментальне питання: кому належить місто і за які можливі траєкторії його майбутнього досі варто боротися? ●

1   Схожі міські процеси відбувалися й деінде. У Детройті 1980-х покинуті будівлі стали прихистком для культурних спільнот, що шукали безпечних просторів, а згодом утворили рух глобального значення. У Берліні після возз'єднання невикористані простори стали поштовхом до виникнення клубної та культурної сцени, що сформувала образ міста і, за даними досліджень, сьогодні приносить понад 1,5 млрд євро щороку.

2   Поняття «симулякр» походить від Жана Бодріяра, який у своїй праці «Симулякри та симуляція» (*Simulacres et Simulation*, 1981) описує, як у постмодерному суспільстві знаки та образи дедалі більше відокремлюються від свого початкового референта — тобто реальності. На місце реального приходить симуляція, яка вже посилається лише на саму себе. У цьому сенсі «симулякр» позначає копію без оригіналу — інсценовану дійсність, що заміщує автентичність.

Аріна Янович — архітекторка та дослідниця, що мешкає в Берліні. Її робота зосереджена на збереженні, активації та трансформації (індустріальних) територій.

Окупаційний рефлекс

Олексій Мінько

Я мушу уникати метафор, говорячи про окупацію. Інакше ризикую втратити право про неї говорити. Зрадити окупацію, здатися перед викликом, який вона становить. Саме цього я навчився в академічного дискурсу та етики дослідження. «Деколонізація — не метафора»[1], тож мені не варто її застосовувати.

Я мушу пам'ятати, як окупанти створюють інфраструктуру, поєднуючи «їхні» та «мої» технології, придивляючись до фактів цієї динаміки. Я мушу їх розрізняти й будувати власну аргументацію, спостерігаючи за російськими слідами на полі бою та окупованих територіях. Я мушу бачити потенціал у практиках і не дозволяти загрозі його перехопити й підпорядкувати російській версії майбутнього. Мені варто бути нейтральним і зосередженим на доказах, утримуючись від перебільшень. Я мушу бути холодним інтерфейсом під час гарячої фази війни. Я мушу уявляти лише те, що чую від рідних та журналістів-розслідувачів. Окупація ліпить мою етику через негативне, через те, що мені не доступне, через те, про що я менше знаю й не маю можливості знати краще та поширювати далі, адже люди, які знаходяться там, опиняться під загрозою[2].

Я мушу мовчати про те, чого не знаю. Коли себе не обмежую, я стаю зрадником. В очах зрадника окупація розгортається з обох боків лінії фронту. Сили оборони не можуть її стримати. Простори, які зайняли росіяни, тепер інші. У них атоми живуть у конвульсіях.

У випадку України есхатологія[3] — це емпірична наука. Кінець світу — це лише низка буденних статистик, ресурсних розрахунків та вдалих або невдалих експериментів з подолання обмежень наявного стану. Я знайду спосіб залишитися холодним.

Зрештою, те, про що я мушу мовчати, я мушу мовчати мовою науки, мовою фактів, переконливих досліджень, суджень і доказів. Замість мови я можу спробувати послуговуватися скигленням жертви, що в агонії повторює слова свого ката. Я пародіюватиму те, що хоче почути вбивця. На його умовах, згідно з його амбіціями. Нехай він переможе. Вбивця так сильно хоче перемогти. Він говоритиме моїм ротом і висловлюватиметься метафорично.

Непокірна собака Павлова⁴. Ця собака буде поводитись як годиться. Ми підготуємо її до нашого прибуття. Вимкніть світло.

Росіяни пересуваються у бронетранспортері біля торгового центру. Перед ним стоїть черга. Всередині немає світла. Люди чекають на «гуманітарну допомогу», що зберігається в приміщенні. Навколо автобуси із встановленими на дахах екранами, де показують, як отримати нові документи, а з ними й нові сімкарти.

З'являється багато невідомих місцевим облич.

Пошкоджені будівлі зносяться і з'являються подібні до них нові — з яскравими барвистими балконами. Поруч з ними — пам'ятники полеглим солдатам. Десь між ними на автомобілі проїжджає диктатор.

Місцеві музеї починають переглядати й реорганізовувати свої експозиції. Залишиться тільки те, що не вдасться перевезти, — самі будівлі, церкви. Мало що зміниться у музеї, присвяченому подіям Другої світової війни. Закреслене маркером нанесеться наново.

Діти часто потрапляють у літні табори, де навчаються тактиці, першій допомозі й основам керування

дронами. Їх вчать змагатися одне з одними. На спеціально побудованому тренувальному полі проведуть турнір. Зі зброєю, військовою технікою, імітацією розриву снарядів, танками, відеотрансляціями та балами, що нараховуються за успішне виконання завдань. Насправді це не літній табір, а військовий полігон для дітей. Наприкінці їхнього (часто примусового) візиту дітей просять поділитися своїми враженнями перед камерою. Вони кажуть, що гарно відпочили й готові знову повернутися в табір. Їхня наступна поїздка відбудеться вже в рамках військової служби.

Спочатку російські попзірки виступатимуть на відкритих сценах. На тлі видно руїни. Основна публіка — це камера, чи радше ті, хто дивитимуться новини. Згодом будуть лише концерти симфонічної музики, день акордеона та дні перемоги навесні, влітку, восени та взимку. Фотографії з цих подій зберігатимуться на безлюдних телеграм-каналах.

Я чекаю на інформацію від друзів щодо подорожі за кордон. Коли я намагаюся, мені не дозволяють виїхати. А потім починаються знайомі обмеження: мобілізація. Добровільна чи примусова — не має значення. Обмеження щодо пересування. «Держава у смартфоні»⁵. Соціальна угода. Соціальна згода. Виборів нема. Вмиватися за наявності електрики. Читати за відсутності електрики.

Собака сидить у темряві.

Репортажі про фільтраційні табори, депортації, перевиховання дітей, виселення українців/-ок з їхніх домівок, тортури, вбивства. Стеження й переслідування, військовий облік. Новини про російські успіхи на фронті. Очікування партнерів/-ок та чоловіків і

дружин активного військового персоналу. Російські обстріли, загиблі. Це окупація авансом

Інформація розповсюджується. Уламки будівельних конструкцій наповнюють кімнату після вибуху. Історія про падіння уламків на будівлю передається із вуст в уста і так далі[6]. Терор і контроль складаються з часток інформаційного пилу. Росіяни викликають демона пилинок і осколків, який у духовному, так і матеріальному вимірах, змітає все живе з поверхні землі. Єдиним рухом своєї лапи він додає їх до своєї конституції.

Якщо окупація відбувається десь, то вона відбувається скрізь. Коли вона приходить, відношення між «тут» і «там» напружуються і не розслабляються. Вони амортизують. Тіла, прив'язані до цих відношень, набрякають[7].

Це суспільство телепатів/-ок. Ті, хто до нього належать, володіють спільним знанням, яке вони проспівують у думки одне одних задля відчуття єдності. Від цього у них болить голова, а в інтервалах між піснями люди починають шепотіти. Вони сумніваються у деяких віршах і сперечаються про їхні інтерпретації та співзвучність. Демон наполегливий, і коли голоси телепатів/-ок зриваються, залишивши по собі тільки шепотіння, його шепіт звучить найгучніше.

Що більше буферних зон створює демон між тим, що відняли і що обороняють, то більша спокуса здатися. В імперіалістичному казино колонізовані змушені робити найвищі ставки, ризикуючи всім. Для внутрішньо переміщених осіб війна — це телекінетичний досвід. Вони тримаються за фізичні об'єкти за багато кілометрів від них, що є їхньою формою спротиву.

Не більше, не менше: зберігати свій віртуальний аватар у ворожому тилу вночі, кожного разу прориваючись крізь демонічний телефронтир.

Вмикай світло. Слина капає?

Сон. Я опиняюся в Москві на кілька днів. Я гуляю по одних і тих самих вулицях, десь не зовсім у центрі міста. Деякі будівлі пошкоджені українськими дронами. Мене турбує, що перехожі зазирнуть у мій телефон, коли у ньому з'явиться повідомлення українською. Люди в автобусі вже помітили мій акцент. Проходячи через парк (чому я тут гуляю, що я повинен тут знайти?), я бачу, як російському чоловікові дають повістку на паралельній вулиці. Те саме може статися зі мною в будь-який момент. Коли звідси від'їжджає мій автобус? Чи перевірятимуть мої документи, коли я їхатиму?

Ще один сон. У Запоріжжі є трохи світла. KFC чомусь відкритий (чи був колись у Запоріжжі KFC, і якщо так, то як він може бути відкритий?). Починає гудіти сирена. Як захиститися від удару КАБом? Поруч є підземний перехід, тож не варто відходити, якщо місто раптом стане мішенню. Я голодний. Коли задзвенить будильник у моєму телефоні?

З точки зору частоти сни про моє рідне місто приходять рідше, ніж сни про Москву. Можливо, сни про окупацію починаються, коли я прокидаюся від звуків обстрілу. Іноді це сни наяву у формі письма, розмови чи перформансу. В такі моменти мені не сниться окупація: я говорю про відстані, часові відмінності, міражі й тривожні передчуття — загалом про стосунки попри перешкоди.

Колись я помітив, що в моєї бабусі під окупацією була не 7 година вечора, як у мене, а, наприклад, 8. Деколи було навпаки: у мене північ, а в неї — 11 ночі. Одного року український час випереджає російський, наступного — навпаки. Різниця може бути не в одну годину, а в декілька. Коли озброєний меридіан розірвав нашу комунікацію, ми з бабусею провели разом більше чи менше часу?

Страх перед неможливістю втекти від російської небезпеки у снах схожий за інтенсивністю на бажання з'їсти хачапурі[8] моєї бабусі. Коли заздвенить будильник?

Ремінці стискають тіло собаки. Вона ворушиться більше.

Мені снились атаки на українські міста й просування у селі на Сумщині, але не снився окупований Київ, Харків або Дніпро. Окупація всієї України може виявитися не такою вже й видовищною. Для декого життя зведеться до переховування й намагання уникнути певних бюрократичних процедур. Інших вона приведе до суду, а згодом до тюремної камери або до швидкої смерті після жорстокого розгону протесту.

Чи наважусь я кинути коктейль Молотова у бронетранспортер на вулиці обласного центру, якщо досі не наважився вступити в бій з боєприпасами, вогнепальною зброєю в руках, артилерією та підтримкою авіації? Чи наважусь я не міняти свій український паспорт на російський, якщо збираюся ухилятись від служби в українській армії після закінчення моєї відстрочки цього літа? Чи наважусь я залишусь, якщо зможу виїхати? Чи зможу я

вчинити самогубство, якщо мене примусово призвуть у російську армію? Чи можливо бути настільки стійким, щоб уникнути колаборації? Чи можливо бути настільки безвідповідальним, щоб на неї погодитись?

Із собаки знімають ремінці. Вона лягає біля ніг свого господаря.

Булгаков невдало завершив «Собаче серце»[9]. У цій історії професор на ім'я Прєображенській перетворює собаку на людину, але після багатьох неприємностей повертає йому собачу подобу. Ось як я це бачу: пес, якого професор перетворив на людину, знайшов спосіб перетворити самого професора на пса. Він навчився виконувати спеціальну операцію й саме так учинив. Навіть під прицілом пістолета пес-професор не ліг на спину на знак покори. Це було частково пов'язано з його аристократичним походженням, а частково — з надокучливими блохами на його шкірі.

Чи справді собаки відчувають провину, коли їх сварять за невиконання команд? А коли їх хвалять, чи дійсно вони цьому радіють? Українську собаку, яку турбує лише те, яка вона особлива і звідки береться їжа, видає її нещира лояльність[10].

Суб'єктом окупації гребують усі, навіть він сам. Росіяни не впевнені у його відданості, тому докладають стільки зусиль, щоб його переконати. У суб'єкті також сумніваються українські захисники/-ці: а раптом суб'єкт перетворився на зрадника? Сам суб'єкт окупації змучений власним вибором залишитися. Змучений, бо в цьому очікуванні може схибити в тому, як демонструє відданість росіянам, або зайде

занадто далеко, граючи роль колаборанта, зрадивши український народ. Його амбівалентність загрожує всім воюючим сторонам. Для цього суб'єкта простір між сумнівом та вибором — субверсивний у будь-якому порядку, який з'явиться з компресії війни.

Звучить свисток. Собаку б'ють струмом. Вона знерухомлена. Чути скиглення. Удари струмом стають сильнішими.

Чи сниться собакам майбутнє? ●

Олексій Мінько — художник і дослідник, учасник дослідницького колективу *Occupational Formations: Infrastructures of the Seen and Unseen.*

 Окупаційний рефлекс

1 «Деколонізація — не метафора» — це академічна стаття Ів Так і К. Вейн-Янга, в якій вони критикують поверхневе розуміння деколонізації та закликають до деколонізації як конкретної дії — повернення окупованої землі корінним народам. Див.: Tuck, Eve; Yang, K. Wayne (2012). "Decolonization is not a metaphor." *Decolonization: Indigeneity, Education & Society*. 1 (1): 1–40.

2 Ці думки — результат наших розмов із Владою Важеєвським в рамках робочої групи *Occupational Formations: Infrastructures of Seen and Unseen.*

3 Есхатологія — теологічна доктрина в монотеїстичних традиціях, що формулює віру в кінцеву долю світу і людства, зокрема кінець світу, Апокаліпсис та судний день.

4 Іван Павлов (14.09.1849 — 27.02.1936) — російський фізіолог, відомий своєю роботою над концепцією умовних рефлексів. Він проводив експерименти на нервовій системі собак. У його найвідомішому експерименті голодну собаку навчили виділяти слину у відповідь на звук дзвінка, який систематично лунав перед годуванням.

5 Це гасло асоціюється з «Дією» — українським застосунком, що робить державні послуги доступними для громадян через їхні смартфони. Коли Міністерство оборони України розробило застосунок для контролю військового призову, фраза, яка раніше асоціювалася з позитивними змінами, тепер використовується в іронічному сенсі.

6 На ці спостереження надихнув текст Світлани Матвієнко «Середовище терору». Див.: *Theater.SpatialTech*. https://theater. spatialtech.info/en/essays/terror-environment.

7 За мотивами лекції Асі Баздирєвої в рамках освітньої програми Валерії Мальченко «Внутрішній геній війни щодень» у співпраці зі спільнотою *workingprogress* (w.i.p).

8 Хачапурі — грузинська страва, яка має кілька варіантів. Зазвичай це хліб, начинений сиром. Здебільшого начиняється сулугуні — еластичним грузинським засоленим сиром.

9 «Собаче серце» — назва роману народженого в Києві письменника Міхаіла Булгакова. Написаний 1925 року роман сатирично зображує раннє радянське суспільство. Роман розповідає про приблудного пса, якого відомий професор-хірург перетворює на людину, а потім назад на собаку через те, що той неетично поводився.

10 В оповіданні Франца Кафки «Дослідження собаки» розповідь ведеться від імені собаки-дослідника, який, зокрема, шукає відповідь на питання, звідки Земля добуває їжу.

Оливки

У цій березневій прозорій імлі, у цій повітряній
    прелюдії квітня,
Коли кожен розцвіте як зможе, у брунатній шухляді
    купе,
такій же лискучій, так-так, як лусочка бруньки,
    маленька дівчинка малювала в альбомі
    «оливки миру»:
Бо хтось колись сказав, що голуб приносив після
    біди
гілочку оливкового дерева, але я думаю, мама, що
    він би міг
принести і цілу банку оливок, тоді б можна було
    зробити салат. Так-так.

Як із прадавніх міфів проступали ці наші суворі
    закинуті села північних країв,
з кошлатими бровами сухостоїв минали поля. До
    півдня було неблизько. Так-так.
До півдня тільки птахи вільно ладнали свої ключі.
    І переможно стояла у повітрі весна.
Своя. Рідна. Виписана таким запаморочливо
    зеленим скорописом по чорних
сторінках згарищ. І голуб літав, і довго не міг знайти
    дику оливку, і приніс-таки
тобі у сон її сріблясту намистину. Так-так.

Юлія Стахівська, 2023

Хроніка воєнного виснаження

Єлизавета Ланденберґер

24 лютого 2022 року, ранок

Я прокидаюся від неспокійного сну близько п'ятої ранку в своїй (колишній) квартирі у Чехії та відразу дивлюся у телефон. Тижнями я була прикута до екрану, безперервно читаючи новини, телеграм-канали, твіттер-треди. Мої найгірші страхи збулися: війна почалася.

Я відчайдушно пишу друзям і подругам в Україні з пропозиціями хоч якоїсь допомоги, а також друзям у Росії з проханням хоч щось зробити.

Згідно з Ганною Арендт, поняття «влади» й «насильства» помилково ототожнюють, коли розглядають насильство як «найгрубший прояв влади»[1].

Арендт не згодна. Насильство застосовують тоді, коли влада розпадається. Насправді це протилежні поняття: «де один є абсоютним правителем, інший — відсутній»[2].

24 лютого 2022 року, вечір

Велика протестна акція у Празі. Люди — з України, Білорусі, Росії, Грузії, але переважно з Чехії — кидають яйця у вітрину навпроти російського посольства, вигукуючи гасла на кшталт «Путін, іди нахуй», поки поліціянти стоять поруч і посміхаються. Хтось обмотав паркан навколо посольства туалетним папером з надрукованим на ньому обличчям Путіна. На банері з вражаючою ясністю написано чеською «*Invaze je zlo*» («Вторгнення — це зло»). У повітрі витає згуртованість, п'янке почуття солідарності, що пронизує та мобілізує тіло і розум. Пам'ять про 1968-й здається живою — Празька весна. Розквіт демократії та її подальше придушення військами Варшавського пакту. Образи радянських танків у Празі не зблякли в спогадах людей навіть через пів століття.

«Насильство [...] вирізняється своїм інструмен-
тальним характером. Феноменологічно воно близьке
до сили, оскільки знаряддя насильства, як і всі інші
інструменти, створені й застосовуються з метою
множення природної сили, аж поки на останній ста-
дії своєї розробки стають здатними її замінити»[3].

Згідно з Арендт, придушення Празької весни
було «хрестоматійним випадком конфронтації між
насильством і владою в їхньому чистому вигляді»[4].

Російське повномасштабне вторгнення — ще
один, і Путін, очевидно, не читав Арендт. Йому не вдалося побудувати фундамент для влади за допомогою
дезінформації, атак і підтримки сепаратистів на сході
та півдні України. Навпаки — Росія ставала там дедалі
непопулярнішою через війну на Донбасі, яка зруйну-
вала сім'ї та знищила безліч життів. Оскільки Путін
не мав влади, він вдався до насильства, помилково
вважаючи, що це найвища форма влади.

25 лютого 2022 року

Після прибуття в Берлін я приголомшена відсутністю війни. Люди на вулицях і в кафе здаються
безтурботними, все виглядає нормальним. Великого
напливу біженців іще не відбулося.

У наступні дні я сортую пожертви для біженців/-
ок. Вони зможуть забезпечити себе найнеобхід-
нішим — снеками, милом, зубними щітками — у
своєрідному безкоштовному магазині. Інші пожертви їдуть на захід України у вантажівках. Деякі
речі, які пожертвували берлінці/-ки, непридатні для
використання. Деякий одяг невипраний і подірявле-
ний. Я натрапляю на старий гребінець, між зубцями
якого застрягли пасма волосся — ніби хтось просто
позбувся тут свого сміття.

27 лютого 2022 року

Велика демонстрація за мир в Україні у центрі Берліна. За даними поліції, взяли участь 100 000 людей, але здавалося, що пів мільйона. Я рада, що німецьке суспільство таки не байдуже до війни.

Потім я бачу плакати, оздоблені голубами, символами миру та гаслами проти зброї, і розумію, що цього дня зібралися дві різні фракції з протилежними цілями. Одна засуджує російське вторгнення і вимагає відповідних санкцій проти агресора. Інші — начебто пацифісти — вважають, що українці повинні здатися.

Вони не розуміють, що означає окупація. На відміну від чехів/-шок, частина німецького населення не зазнала насильсва радянського панування. Інша частина — зі Сходу — здається, часто занурюється в ностальгію, забувши про реалії тоталітаризму.

30 листопада 2022 року

Там, звідки відступають російські війська, пізніше стає зрозуміло, на які звірства вони здатні: на вулицях Бучі, в лісах Ізюма, камерах тортур у Херсоні.

17 жовтня 2023 року

У Берлінському літературному домі власник і видавець лівого тижневика *Der Freitag* Якоб Ауґштайн розмовляє з Танею Малярчук – українською письменницею, яка мешкає у Відні. Я слухаю їхню розмову по радіо. Зарозумілість Ауґштайна викликає у мене іспанський сором:

«У мене завжди було відчуття, що я живу в травмованому, пораненому місті. [...] У мого померлого батька був дивний шрам на руці. Тут була вхідна рана, а з іншого боку — вихідна рана [...] Війна була присутня в нашому житті, у моєму житті. Ви, мабуть,

думаєте, що маєте справу з якимось розпещеним, слабким західним засранцем. Але ви не знаєте, що означає війна в моїй біографії, моєму минулому, так би мовити. [...] Це означає, що я дійсно, по-справжньому боюся війни, справді боюся».

Ауґштайн використовує свою позицію публічного мовця, щоб підкреслити, наскільки важливо уникнути ескалації війни. Але найморошнішими є його коментарі щодо Парижа: яке щастя, що його не захищали у військовий спосіб під час Другої світової війни, бо інакше міста би вже не існувало. Він вважає, що Київ теж не повинен захищатися, а натомість має бути завойований.

Мабуть, він не усвідомлює, що саме німці під час Другої світової війни перетворили на руїни і попіл значну частину сучасної України, тому його аналогія виглядає доволі викривленою. Основне послання Ауґштайна таке: я втомився від війни і боюся. Припиніть її та дайте мені хоч трохи спокою.

Ауґштайн настільки еґоцентричний, що не звертає уваги на те, як почувається його співрозмовниця, яка безпосередньо переживає війну.

26 серпня 2024 року

Сара Ваґенкнехт, тодішня лідерка власної однойменної партії BSW[5], їздить по східній Німеччині напередодні виборів. Сьогодні вона виступає у своєму рідному місті Єні. «І де нам також потрібні фундаментальні зміни — і я це беру справді близько до серця, — це у питаннях війни і миру!» — вигукує вона перед завзятим натовпом.

Я тут як журналістка. Роздають листівки російською, мабуть, націлені на таких, як я — етнічних німців, що переїхали до Німеччини у 1990-х.

Рішення, які пропонують популісти, прості: зниження оренди, підняття пенсії. Ні війні, миру — так. Ніякої зброї Україні, отже, мир.

Наприкінці промови — несподіванка: українські жінки стають навпроти сцени із синьо-жовтими плакатами й вигукують «Підтримайте Україну!» та «Зупиніть російську агресію!». Перевірка реальністю для присутніх. Вони освистують біженок та ображають їх: «Волоцюги!», «Вертайтесь додому!», «Мілітаристки!». Лише завдяки поліції вони не вдаються до насильства. Присутність жертв війни привносить реальність у зачаровані голови прихильників/-ць Ваґенкнехт, загрожуючи зруйнувати їхній світогляд, тож вони чинять опір.

Того ж дня Україна потерпає від одного з найжорстокіших російських авіаударів.

2 березня 2025 року

«Я це називаю покровською дієтою — 17 кілограмів за 0,2 секунди», — жартує Едді Скотт на своєму лікарняному ліжку. Едді — цивільний, волонтер. У складі ГО BaseUA він евакуював людей із прифронтових територій. Я відвідую його в київській лікарні як журналістка. Він втомлений, втратив ліву ногу та ліву руку після удару російського FPV-дрона в Донецькій області. Каже, що впоратись йому допомагає чорний гумор.

Те, що сталося з Едді, — будні українських цивільних. Кожен такий інцидент мав би нас шокувати, але здається, дедалі менше людей справді щось помічають. Згідно з німецьким дослідженням, старші виборці та люди з обмеженими політичними інтересами більш схильні до воєнної втоми і скептицизму щодо тривалих військових операцій[6].

10 серпня 2025 року

Чекаючи на піцу в Берліні, я читаю новини в інстаграмі: художник Давид Чичкан загинув на фронті. Я не можу повірити. Всього тиждень тому він відправив мені голосове повідомлення, яке я слухаю знову і знову. Новий матеріал, який я мала написати про нього, ніколи не буде написаний. Натомість я пишу некролог крізь сльози.

2 жовтня 2025 року

Я думаю про Маріуполь — портове місто, зруйноване російськими військами у перші місяці війни. Дослідження гуманітарних організацій свідчать, що з березня 2022 року по лютий 2023 року було поховано понад 10 000 осіб, причому щонайменше 8000 з них загинули в результаті бойових дій або пов'язаних з війною причин. Фактична кількість жертв, імовірно, набагато більша, оскільки незліченну кількість загиблих не знайшли під завалами. Росія буквально відновлює місто на кістках колишніх мешканців/-ок.

Токшоу, «демонстрації за мир» та як ліві, так і праві медіа, що відмовляються проявляти будь-яку солідарність з українцями/-ками, часто використовують таке слово, як «мілітарист» або його синонім «беліцист» (від лат. *bellicus* — «військовий», «воєнний», — Прим. перекл.). Ці терміни зазвичай застосовують, щоб образити українців/-ок або людей, солідарних із країною, що зазнала вторгнення, які вимагають конкретних наслідків для Росії. Іншим поняттям у цьому списку є «воєнне виснаження» у тому сенсі, в якому його найчастіше використовують.

«Ми втомились від війни!» — пишуть у соцмережах лівої партії *Die Linke* у Саксонії на початку вересня. Стверджують, що миру не досягти через

поставки зброї, а лише через дипломатію, роззбро-
єння та міжнародну співпрацю. Як же це має спра-
цювати, якщо агресор взагалі не зацікавлений
у мирі?

Утім, зумовлене медіа воєнне виснаження
здається неминучим, людським: щодня ми бачимо
зображення вигорілих будинків та мертвих пей-
зажів, військових з брудними обличчями та втом-
леними очима. Ми читаємо й чуємо ті самі історії
насильства, страждань і злочинів — знову і знову. Не
лише в Україні, але й в інших місцях по всьому світу.
Хто досі сприймає цю інформацію, хто досі нею
переймається?

Водночас російська військова економіка працює
на повну, й авіаудари по містах і цивільній інфраструктурі частішають. Села навіть за 20 кілометрів
від фронту стали непридатними для проживання.
Російська армія запускає дедалі більше квадротор-
них дронів, оснащених вибухівкою, які полюють
на все, що рухається.

Ми часто чуємо, що люди в Україні стомились
від війни. І так, вони виснажені вже давно. Але що
їм робити?

Заміна влади насильством може принести пере-
могу, але ціна занадто висока, пише Арендт. «Адже
її сплачують не лише переможені, але й переможці,
втрачаючи владу». Вона стверджує: «Насильство
може знищити владу, проте воно зовсім не здатне
її створити»[7] ●

Єлизавета Ланденберґер — асистентка-дослідниця в Інституті сла-
вістики та угористики Берлінського університету імені Гумбольдта та
фриланс-журналістка.

1 Hannah Arendt, "On Violence," San Diego / New York / London, 1970, p. 38.

2 p. 56.

3 p. 46.

4 p. 53.

5 Авторитарна ліва партія, заснована 2024 року.

6 https://www.dkjs.de/wp-content/uploads/2025/02/analyse-politische-einstellungen-und-wahlverhalten-junger-menschen.pdf.

7 Arendt, p. 53.

Міський путівник воєнного часу

Олександр Бурлака

Цей текст — короткий путівник моїм рідним містом Києвом, заснований на подіях російської спроби вторгнення у березні 2022 року. Деякі теми важливі й привертають більше уваги, інші згадуються лише побіжно. Варто пам'ятати, що ситуація продовжує змінюватися, поки ви читаєте цей путівник.

Тривога й укриття

Поки я це пишу, міська адміністрація оголосила, що почне встановлювати мобільні укриття. Ці базові бетонні структури стали звичним видовищем на вулицях Харкова, Сум та Дніпра — міст, розташованих ближче до російського кордону чи до лінії фронту. Хоча ці модульні бетонні укриття стають у пригоді як тимчасові захисні структури, вони насамперед функціонують як видимі маркери стану війни. Вони не є всюди обов'язковими, й наразі немає стандартів регулювання їхнього розміру та вмістимості. Як архітектор-поціновувач бруталістстських бетонних форм я вважаю, що ці структури залишаються візуально незавершеними, й оздоблення їх муралами ситуацію не покращує. Дивно, що водночас у місто повертається скло: відбудовують скляні автобусні зупинки, ремонтують фасади й навіть на популярному Скляному мості, що постраждав від ракетного удару у травні 2023 року, протягом місяця замінили прозорі панелі. Є певна зухвалість у тому, як швидко повертається скло, наче місто відмовляє руйнуванню у диктуванні його зовнішнього вигляду. Проте там, де вибухи відбуваються регулярно, скло замінюють на ОСБ-панелі, які швидко й без зайвого клопоту закривають розбиті отвори.

Побудоване в розпал Холодної війни, київське метро було спроєктоване як ефективне укриття на

випадок ядерного удару, з усією необхідною інфраструктурою. Розташоване глибоко під землею, воно обладнане захисними замками та фонтанами з питною водою — деталі, що до 2022 року були практично невідомі. Під час повітряних тривог підземна частина метро відкрита і доступна для безкоштовного користування. У разі удару балістичними ракетами доступ до такого укриття забезпечує відчутний комфорт. Залежно від ситуації, деякі мешканці Києва заздалегідь приходять до метро, щоб провести там ніч, приносячи з собою домашніх тварин, розкладні стільці та необхідні речі.

Утім, є одна проблема — місто суттєво розрослося з часів побудови метро, тож багато районів уже не знаходяться в межах досяжності глибокої станції. До того ж річка розділяє місто на дві частини, й мости, що їх з'єднують, є стратегічними об'єктами. Під час тривог мости закриті. У багатьох нових районах, зокрема на лівому березі, основними укриттями слугують паркувальні споруди — вбудовані гаражі чи підземні паркінги. Різноманітні підвали, наприклад підвали барів та офісів, також залишаються відкритими під час повітряних тривог.

Проте більшість містян/-ок залишаються вдома. Крім заклеювання вікон, багато людей покладаються на «правило ймовірності» (ідею того, що ймовірність потрапляння снаряду в певну квартиру у великому місті доволі низька). Вони також дотримуються «правила двох стін»: згідно з цією теорією, найбезпечніше перебувати в глибині будівлі, переважно в коридорі чи ванній кімнаті, де зовнішня стіна та одна чи дві внутрішні стіни можуть пом'якшити вибухову хвилю або зупинити осколки. Рівень захисту залежить від будівлі та природи удару, але коридор

забезпечує кращий захист, ніж кімната з вікнами. Після численних безсонних ночей люди часто вдаються до використання берушів або навушників, повністю ігноруючи заходи безпеки.

Очевидно, що ця війна виглядає зовсім не так, як ми звикли бачити у фільмах. Лінія фронту — це вже не єдина межа, а радше територія невизначеності, зона ураження, що простягається вглиб на кілометри. Те, як люди реагують на тривоги, часто залежить від потенційного типу удару. Є багато можливостей: підтверджена загроза удару балістичною ракетою, зліт літака, залп крилатих ракет або виявлення ударних і розвідувальних дронів. У прифронтових чи прикордонних регіонах цей спектр загроз є ще ширшим.

Я пишу ці рядки, коли внаслідок масштабного удару по енергетичній інфраструктурі припинено постачання електроенергії та води. Метро на лівому березі не працює.

У медіа повідомляють про підземні станції та резервні батареї. У новинах показують окремі теплоелектростанції, огорнуті сітками та металевими кріпленнями, — образ, що має створювати враження про підготовленість. Проте на поверхні київські станції виглядають майже як завжди. Електроенергія постачається за графіком, іноді лише по кілька годин на день. Усі бізнеси працюють на генераторах, тож під час блекаутів вулиці наповнюються низьким і гучним гудінням. Увечері вуличні ліхтарі не вмикаються, а будинки стоять неосвітлені, наче скелі. Люди купують батареї різної ємності, щоб забезпечити електроенергією побутові прилади та холодильники, а деколи й цілі квартири. Вони встановлюють інвертори та сонячні панелі.

Вони прокладають оптоволоконні інтернет-кабелі та підключають резервні батареї до своїх маршрутизаторів. За останні 20 років середня висота нових житлових будинків зросла до 30 поверхів. Однак під час відключення електроенергії ліфти не працюють.

Пам'ять і меморіалізація

За майже чотири роки війни почали з'являтися нові пам'ятники та практики пам'яті. Багато з них — народні, інші створюють місцеві адміністрації.

Спочатку на кладовищах почали з'являтися прапори, встановлені на могилах загиблих на фронті. Своїм тріпотінням на вітрі вони порушують спокій кладовища. У селі Мощун поблизу Києва меморіал складається з портретів померлих, прикріплених до обгорілих соснових стовбурів. Аудіозапис тихо перелічує імена військових, які загинули, захищаючи село. Інші місцеві адміністрації швидко вдалися до замовлення муралів.

2023 року громадськості представили черговий меморіал — фотореалістичну пластикову фігуру, присвячену військовому, страту якого після захоплення в полон зняли на відео російські війська. Її реалістичний вигляд бентежить. Проте найсимволічніший імпровізований меморіал постав на київському Майдані Незалежності. Він розпочався з кількох прапорців на галявині, які згодом розповсюдились по всій площі. Тут також відбуваються прощання з тими військовими, які не дотримувалися церковних традицій, були — або не були — важливими публічними фігурами. Серед тих, кого вшановували, — командир батальйону «Вовки Да Вінчі» Дмитро Коцюбайло, Шура Рязанцева й Давид Чичкан — анархіст і художник, чия робота супроводжує цю публікацію.

Такі форми публічної скорботи, доповнені музикою і димовими шашками, стали новою українською традицією. Можливо, це навіть важливіше, ніж пам'ятники, оскільки розширює давню практику зібрань і демонстрацій на громадських площах.

Останнім часом дотримання хвилини мовчання стало рутиною в публічних просторах. Оголошення та різноманітні сигнали стали ще одним елементом звукового ландшафту України, як і виття сирен. Люди встають у швидкісних поїздах та на перехрестях, автомобілі зупиняються в центрі міста.

Ринок нерухомості

Рієлтори — найоптимістичніша соціальна група. Кожну новину, офіційну заяву чи незначну зміну вони сприймають як потенційну ознаку стабільності й потенційне зростання ціни оренди.

У лютому 2022 року ціни впали й багато договорів було розірвано. Хоча Київ — столиця України, системи підтримки внутрішньо переміщених осіб (ВПО) немає. Такі інституції існують у кожному регіональному центрі, але не тут. За словами заступника міністра розвитку громад та територій України, станом на 25 жовтня в Києві проживало 400 000 ВПО — один із найвищих показників у країні. Однак обсяг будівництва житла в Києві зараз утричі нижчий, ніж торік, і лише третина цього обсягу припадає на державну програму доступного житла, що дозволяє українцям купувати квартири за пільговими іпотечними ставками — від 3% для військовослужбовців до 7% для ВПО.

За останні десять років через окупацію та подальше поширення бойових дій відбулося кілька хвиль внутрішнього переміщення. Люди з

високооплачуваними роботами часто переїжджа-
ють до Києва, спричиняючи зростання цін. Іншим
фактором є статистична нерівномірність: деякі
райони обстрілюють частіше, тож вони є небезпечні-
шими. Серед них, наприклад, Солом'янський район
і місцевість навколо станції метро «Лук'янівська», де
розташовані великі військові виробничі об'єкти. Хоча
в цих кварталах може бути більше варіантів оренди
житла або офісних приміщень, варто бути готовими
до того, що іноді доведеться заміняти розбиті вікна.

Блокпости й протести

Блокпости контролюють головні в'їзні та виїзні
дороги на околицях міста. Там поліція проводить
довільні перевірки документів і вантажів. Схожі
перевірки відбуваються також на входах до залізничних вокзалів. Оскільки залізниця працює вночі,
вона стала основним видом транспорту. З півночі до
п'ятої ранку діє комендантська година, під час якої
заборонено пересування без спеціального дозволу.

На початку вторгнення численні імпровізовані
блокпости з'являлися по всій країні внаслідок паніч-
них настроїв. Кожна громада очікувала на прибуття
колон російських танків, тож на дорожні знаки
наносили протитанкові послання, а також поспіхом
споруджували металеві бар'єри. Комендантська
година починалася о 20:00 й іноді тривала кілька
днів. Сьогодні блокпости та комендантська година
нагадують радше формальність, спрямовану на
підтримання дисципліни в суспільстві. Вона існує
поряд із забороною мітингів. Однак протести, здається, стали частиною української суспільної ідентичності. Після ухвалення влітку та восени кількох
суперечливих законів, що обмежують незалежність

антикорупційних органів та посилюють покарання для звичайних військовослужбовців, відбулася низка неоголошених демонстрацій.

Головним місцем для зібрання протестувальників/-ць стала площа перед Театром Франка, звідки наразі відкривається найкращий вид на будівлю Офісу Президента. Мітинги відбувалися навіть навпроти парламенту — на одній з найбільш контрольованих територій урядового кварталу.

Рушійною силою цієї нової протестної культури стали люди, які під час революції на Майдані у 2013–2014 роках були дітьми. Вони розробили нову протестну мову: химерні, іронічні та мемоподібні висловлювання на картонках, у яких політична реальність сплітається з інтернет-культурою.

Видимість нормальності

Загалом міська тканина змінювалася поступово. Після ночі в укритті люди або йдуть на роботу, або працюють з дому. Деякі чоловіки не виходять, боячись мобілізації на вулиці, поки інші доставляють їм продукти. Утім, деякі досі мобілізуються добровільно.

Сьогодні армія пропонує широкий спектр можливостей працевлаштування на позиції на кшталт перукаря/-ки, кухаря/-ки, відеоредактора/-ки та програміста/-ки. Завдяки численному невійськовому персоналу армія стала ще одним сектором економіки з конкуренцією та складною структурою. Багато людей працюють у сферах, що поєднують військову службу з віддаленою роботою. З'явилося кілька невеликих стартапів у сфері військових технологій, які виробляють дрони та радіоелектроніку. Інші компанії фокусуються на легких у

конструюванні модульних будинках, гнучких рішеннях для відбудови й 3D-друці для швидкої відбудови критичної інфраструктури.

Уроки для майбутнього

У час, коли безглузді війни можуть раптово спалахнути, відкидаючи звичні правила, постає питання: чого ми можемо навчитися на основі цього досвіду з перспективи міського планування? Коли 2022 року я був у австрійському місті Ґрац, де народилася моя донька, мешканці/-ки місцевого житлового комплексу обговорювали, як підготуватися до блекауту. Деякі встановили сонячні панелі на своїх терасах. Тоді мені це здавалося надмірною обережністю. Але тепер я думаю, що цього недостатньо.

Одним із пріоритетів має бути захист інфраструктури через створення незалежних мереж електропостачання, опалення та водопостачання. Не менш важливою є і пожежна безпека, оскільки багато людей гинуть радше від спричинених ударами пожеж, ніж від самих ударів. Якість будівництва також має значення. Хоча побудувати ідеальні сховища неможливо, варто вивчати споруди й структури, а також розробляти плани швидкої трансформації перших поверхів і великих внутрішніх просторів в укриття.

Після тривалого спостереження за наслідками дронових і ракетних ударів стає зрозуміло, як різні конструктивні системи реагують на руйнування. Послідовний план управління цими ризиками захистив би мешканців/-ок і зміцнив довіру до державних інститутів та країни в цілому.

Якщо Україна виживе в цій війні, нам доведеться змінити пріоритети у сфері забудови. Замість

зосереджуватися на оформленні й репрезентації перевагу варто надати безпеці людей та довкілля. Іншим ключовим принципом має бути доступність, тобто фізичні умови, що дозволяють користуватися публічними просторами всім — зокрема людям, що втратили кінцівки чи зір.

Суспільство бореться зі страхом, болем і незручностями, але кияни все одно ходять у ресторани, на вечірки, концерти, вистави та виставки, збираються в кафе і на громадських площах.

Дивлячись у майбутнє, органи влади мають сфокусуватися на колективній взаємодії та соціальній інфраструктурі. Замість романтизувати минуле та звеличувати війну й героїзм потрібні спільні зусилля для забезпечення тих речей, які роблять місто дійсно придатним для життя: повага до всіх живих істот у його межах. Це вимагатиме уваги як до великого, так і до малого, до минулого і до сьогодення ●

Олександр Бурлака — архітектор і фотограф, фокус роботи якого — міське планування та трансформації, що відбуваються в Україні сьогодні.

Особлива подяка:
Рувен Брюес
Женя Дворецька
Анна Кьоніг
Фабіан Мюльталер
Марія Шубчик

Нотатки про життя
Роздуми про сучасну Україну

Редактор: Макс Ойліц
Графічний дизайн: Лоренц Клінґебіль
Літографія: Олексій Новіков
Переклад: Юстина Кравчук,
Саша Місюра
Літературне редагування: Зої Філд
Коректура: Еймс Джероулд,
Ірина Ніколайчук
Друк: Westermann Druck Zwickau
Шрифт: ABC Favorit (Dinamo)

Видавництво: Spector Books
Verlagsgesellschaft mbH
Harkortstraße 10
04107 Leipzig
www.spectorbooks.com

Дистрибуція:
Німеччина, Австрія: GVA,
Gemeinsame Verlagsauslieferung
Göttingen GmbH & Co. KG,
www.gva-verlage.de
Швейцарія: AVA Verlagsauslieferung
AG, www.ava.ch
Франція, Бельгія: Interart Paris,
www.interart.fr
Велика Британія: Central Books Ltd,
www.centralbooks.com
США, Канада, Центральна та
Південна Америка, Африка:
ARTBOOK/D.A.P., www.artbook.com
Японія: twelvebooks,
www.twelve-books.com
Південна Корея: The Book Society,
www.thebooksociety.org
Австралія, Нова Зеландія:
Perimeter Distribution,
www.perimeterdistribution.com

© 2026, автори, редактори та Spector
Books, Leipzig

Перше видання: 2026

Надруковано в ЄС
ISBN 978-3-95905-950-3

Підписи до зображень

Маргарита Половінько (1994–2025)

Сторінка 13, із серії
«Ангели 502», 2023,
папір та олівець

Сторінка 22, Без назви
(фрагмент), бл. 2022–23,
кров на папері

Сторінка 36, із серії
«Ангели 502», 2023,
папір та олівець

Сторінка 45, *Без назви*, 2022,
кров на папері

Сторінка 60, *Без назви*, 2022,
кров на папері

Сторінка 77, із серії
«Ангели 502» (фрагмент), 2023,
папір та олівець

Сторінка 84, *Без назви*, 2022,
кров на папері

Сторінка 95, *Без назви*
(фрагмент), 2022,

кров на папері

Сторінка 105, *Без назви*, 2022,

кров на папері

Сторінка 111, із серії
«Ангели 502», 2023,
папір та олівець

Сторінка 116, *Без назви*
(фрагмент), 2022,

кров на папері

Обкладинка: обидві роботи
з серії

«Ангели 502», 2023,
папір та олівець

Англомовна частина

Усі роботи сфотографовані Віктором Павленком.
Надано зі згоди спадкоємців Маргарити Половінько.

Давид Чичкан (1986–2025)

Сторінки 14, 25, 39, 47, 78, 87, 98,
109 *Без назви* (Зі стрічками та
прапорами), акварель на папері,
86 × 61 cm, 2022–24

Україномовна частина